THE THINGS OUR FATHERS SAW

THE UNTOLD STORIES OF THE
WORLD WAR II GENERATION
FROM HOMETOWN, USA

VOLUME I:
VOICES OF THE PACIFIC THEATER

Matthew A. Rozell

WOODCHUCK HOLLOW PRESS

Hartford · New York

Information at matthewrozellbooks.com

Maps by Susan Winchell.

Photographic portraits of Robert Addison, Daniel Lawler, Dante Orsini and Gerald West used courtesy of Robert H. Miller.

Front Cover: "Marines Under Fire, Tarawa, November 1943". Official USMC photograph. USMC Archives. Used with permission.

Back Cover: 27th Infantry Division, Saipan, July 1944. Signal Corps., United States Army. New York State Military Museum. Used with permission.

Publisher's Cataloging-in-Publication Data

Names: Rozell, Matthew A., 1961-
Title: The things our fathers saw: the untold stories of the World War II generation from hometown, USA-voices of the Pacific Theater / Matthew A. Rozell.
Description: Hartford, NY: Woodchuck Hollow Press, 2015. | Series: The untold stories of the World War II generation from hometown, USA-voices of the Pacific Theater, vol. 1. | Includes bibliographical references.
Identifiers: LCCN 2015920700 | ISBN 978-0-9964800-0-0 (pbk.) | ISBN 978-1-948155-04-5 (hbk.) | ISBN 978-0-9964800-1-7 (ebook)
Subjects: LCSH: World War, 1939-1945--Personal narratives, American. | World War, 1939-1945--Campaigns--Pacific Ocean. | United States. Marine Corps--Biography. | Military history, Modern--20th century. | BISAC: HISTORY / Military / Veterans. | HISTORY / Military / World War II.
Classification: LCC D810.V42 R69 2015 (print) | LCC D810.V42 (ebook) | DDC 940.54/8173--dc23.

matthewrozellbooks.com

Printed in the United States of America

THE THINGS OUR FATHERS SAW

For the mothers who saw their children off to war,
And for those who keep the memory alive.

27th Infantry Division. Saipan, July 1944.
'An abandoned Japanese baby is adopted by front line medical unit of the
27th Div. The baby was found with a scalp wound, in the arms of its dead
mother, by a tank crew during the fighting below Mt. Tapotchau.'
New York State Military Museum.

Dying for freedom isn't the worst that could happen.
Being forgotten is.

— SUSIE STEPHENS-HARVEY, REFLECTING ON HER BROTHER,
STEPHEN J. GEIST
MIA 9-26-1967

I hope you'll never have to tell a story like this,
when you get to be 87.
I hope you'll never have to do it.

— MARINE VETERAN OF THE 1945 BATTLE OF IWO JIMA
TO HIS TEENAGE INTERVIEWER

THE THINGS OUR FATHERS SAW

THE STORYTELLERS (IN ORDER OF APPEARANCE):

HARRY 'RANDY' HOLMES

GERALD ROSS

JOSEPH FIORE

DANTE ORSINI

JOSEPH MINDER

RICHARD M. GORDON

DOROTHY SCHECHTER

JOHN A. LEARY

ROBERT ADDISON

GERALD WEST

THOMAS H. JONES

ALVIN PEACHMAN

JOHN PARSONS

RALPH LEINOFF

WALTER HOOKE

IRVING SCHECHTER

NICHOLAS GRINALDO

JOHN SIDUR

DANIEL LAWLER

JOHN MURRAY

JAMES BUTTERFIELD

ROBERT BLAKESLEE

SANFORD BERKMAN

ARTHUR LaPORTE

HERBERT ALTSHULER

WALTER HAMMER

ANDY DOTY

BRUCE MANELL

KATHERINE ABBOTT

MARY BUTTERFIELD

JOHN NORTON

JOSEPH MARCINO

THE THINGS OUR FATHERS SAW

TABLE OF CONTENTS

Preface

In the study of World War II, we are tempted to teach and learn the history as if the way things turned out was somehow preordained, as if it was a foregone conclusion that Americans and their allies were destined to win the war from the outset. Because we know how events turned out, we tend to read the history with a sense of inevitability. Nothing could be further from the truth. By listening to persons who lived through these troubling times, we gain critical insights that make the study of the past all the more relevant; indeed, I would argue, more urgent. More importantly, their recollections amplify crucial points that should be essential to our understanding of World War II, but are often overlooked.

It is easy to forget that during World War II the United States would be essentially engaging in two full-blown wars at the same time, taxing America's resources and families to the hilt. Many had expected to be in the fight sooner or later in Europe, where it had raged for two years; few expected it to begin in the Pacific. But that is where the story of American involvement begins, and it is also where it would end.

So imagine your world now, and turn it upside down. In this narrative, we focus on the stories of the Pacific War as told by more than 30 survivors who were fortunate enough to return. This is what they saw and brought back with them to the communities surrounding "Hometown, USA."

General Electric's Fort Edward plant is the only completely government-financed factory in the Glens Falls area. A half of its workers live in Glens Falls.   Above, Jean Fitzgerald, Eleanor Penders, Phoebe Francato and Ruth Lopen test synchronous motors for automatic gun turrets on our largest bombers.

'General Electric's Fort Edward plant is the only completely government-financed factory in the Glens Falls area. A half of its workers live in Glens Falls. Above, Jean Fitzgerald, Eleanor Penders, Phoebe Francato and Ruth Lopen test synchronous motors for automatic gun turrets on our largest bombers.'
LOOK Magazine, 1944.[1]

---

[1] Fort Edward High School's sports teams are still known as the "Flying Forts," after the Boeing B-17 Flying Fortress heavy bomber and the motors for the gun turrets built here.

Hometown, USA

During the greatest conflict humanity has ever known, a cluster of small towns in upstate New York sent its sons and daughters off to war. In 1945, after six years of savage fighting, the devastation was unprecedented and incalculable. Between sixty and eighty-five million people—the exact figure will never be known—would be dead. Overseas, the victors would be forced to deal with rubble-choked cities and tens of millions of people on the move, their every step dogged with desperation, famine, and moral confusion. American servicemen, battle-hardened but weary, would be forced to deal with the collapse of civilization and brutally confronted with the evidence of industrial-scale genocide.

John Norton, American sailor at Hiroshima, after the atomic bombing: We walked around. The people, the civilians, were looking at us wondering what we were going to do to them. And, oh my God, the scars on their faces and burns. Oh God, it was sickening. Women and children—it was just sickening.

World War II would become the gatepost on which the rest of the twentieth century would swing.

Just what did our fathers see?

*

In the study of World War II, we are tempted to teach and learn the history as if the way things turned out was somehow preordained, as if it was a foregone conclusion that Americans and their allies were destined to win the war from the outset. As historian (and Pacific Marine veteran) William Manchester noted, because we know how events turned out, we tend to read the history with a sense of inevitability. Nothing could be further from the truth. It is easy to forget that during World War II the United States would be essentially engaging in two full-blown wars at the same time, taxing America's resources and families to the hilt. The story of World War II has been told many times, but only recently have we allowed those who actually lived it to speak for themselves. The narratives in this book are reflective of many of the places in the United States 75 years ago, but most have never been heard before. Most of them are drawn from those who share a connection to the communities surrounding the 'Falls' in the Hudson River, some 200 miles north of where the river joins the sea at New York City. Over a span of six months in 1943 and 1944, *LOOK Magazine* dispatched a team of photographers to Glens Falls, New York, and its environs for a patriotic six-article series on life in what was then dubbed 'Hometown, USA' to a national audience.[2]

---

[2] Assistant Secretary of War Robert P. Patterson had a hand in influencing the selection of the Glens Falls region by the magazine's editors. Born in Glens Falls in 1891, Patterson allegedly helped to steer the magazine towards the North Country in promising the availability of color film, which at the time was scarce and prioritized for military use. Over 5000 photographs were taken by magazine photographers presenting Glens Falls as a model of the home front during World War II.

'Near Falls-Finch, Pruyn & Co., Inc. on Left'
Glens Falls-Hometown USA—LOOK Magazine, 1943-44.
Credit: Crandall Public Library, Folklife Center, Glens Falls N.Y.

Esthetically and demographically, it seemed an apt decision. The counties on the waterfalls on the Hudson River, Washington and Warren, give rise to the Adirondack Mountains and the pristine waters of Lake George to the north. To the east lay Lake Champlain and the Green Mountains of Vermont; just to the south, Saratoga with its historic racetrack, a summertime destination for over 100 years. Beyond Saratoga lay the industrial city of Troy and the state capital of Albany, less than an hour away by rail or automobile. In the early days these counties played pivotal roles in the formation of the United States, given their geographic strategic importance on the Great Warpath, the almost unbroken stretch of water linking New York City with Canada. It was around the vicinity of the 'Falls' that watercraft had to be taken out and portaged. Two major fortifications were constructed here by the British during the French and Indian War, and this was the setting for James Fenimore

Cooper's classic *The Last of the Mohicans*. Half a generation later, a British army sweeping through here would be repulsed by county sons at the Battle of Saratoga.

Following the American Revolution, the early settlers engaged in agricultural pursuits such as dairy farming and, later, sheep raising. Mill-based operations on the river were centered around the upper falls at Glens Falls and the lower falls just downstream at Hudson Falls and evolved into significant lumber and papermaking operations. With the opening of the Erie and Champlain Canals two generations after the Revolution, new worlds opened up, but the 'North Country' counties remained relatively small in population. Living here required hard work in all four seasons, but it was a quiet, close-knit place to raise a family, like many rural areas across America.

Then the war came.

*

Like most every other community in America, from the outside this region seemed untouched by the war. As documented by *LOOK*, life went on to its rhythmic beat—children went off to school, the mills hummed, department stores filled their storefront windows, and farmers sowed and reaped according to the seasons. The beat quickened as young men and women stirred to volunteer, notices arrived in the post box, and many left town for the first time in their lives. Life went on but was now accentuated by rationing, victory gardens, blackouts, and paper and scrap drives. Soon, the arrival of telegrams announcing sons missing or captured, teary phone calls from military hospitals, or worse, the static rings of the front porch doorbell would drive this war home into the heart of 'Hometown, USA' with the fury of hammer blows. Things would never be the same again. Like the 'hard times' of the Great Depression in the preceding decade, this war affected every family. Few American communities would remain unscathed by the emotional detritus of World War II.

Glens Falls-Hometown USA—LOOK Magazine, 1943-44.
Credit: Crandall Public Library, Folklife Center, Glens Falls N.Y.

John Norton: There was a family that lost two sons in World War II. The family got a telegram on a Monday that one of the boys was killed, and that Thursday they got another telegram saying that his brother had been killed. There were about 35 young men from [this town] who were killed in World War II, and I knew every one of them.

Thus the war came and went. Of the sixteen million Americans who donned uniforms, nearly three-quarters of them went overseas. Most returned home to a nation on the cusp of a change not imaginable to their younger selves who had struggled through the Great Depression. The GI Bill of Rights brought new opportunities everywhere, and the economy began to boom. It was best to forget the war and to get on with normal life.

Art LaPorte, U.S. Marine at Iwo Jima: I've had a nightmare down through the years. When I worked at the paper mill sometimes I would be working on something, with all the noise and whatnot, and I would go back in the battles and I could almost smell the gunpowder. I would see all the action for a few seconds. If you had waved your hand in front of me, I would not have known you were there. I was right back there.

'Normal' life. Except maybe it was not going to be that easy.

*

Twilight

Nearly seventy-five years after the beginning of those dark days, the twilight of living memory is now at hand. Day after day we open the newspaper to see that more American veterans have passed on, and we are suddenly on the other side of the 'bell curve' of deaths per day—the downhill slope. By September 30, 2018, the U.S. Department of Veterans Affairs estimates that fewer than 450,000 will remain with us; in just 20 years, the World War II generation will have all gone the way of the veterans of World War I and the Civil War.

I don't know exactly when I was struck by the notion that this day would come, though on some cosmic level I have been planning for it for years. I was born sixteen years after the killing stopped, and I grew up in the company of men and women who fought in World War II. Probably like most kids my age, I had no idea what they did, and like most kids, I did not think to ask. I was raised in this sleepy hamlet on the 'Falls' in many ways not unlike their generation: an innocent in an intact home surrounded by brothers and sisters and community-minded parents. I seemed to draw strength from the study of history at a young age, spending my summer mornings wandering in the woods down near the waterfalls that gave the town its name, searching for evidence of colonial skirmishes and settlements of the French and Indian War and the American Revolution. As I got older I became interested in the conflicts of the twentieth century but remained blissfully unaware of the veterans who were all around me. Some of my teachers in school were veterans of World War II, but I don't remember anyone ever specifically launching into a story about their time in the conflict. It's also possible that they did, but I was not paying attention.

In the late spring of 1984, all of that would change. On television I watched as the 40th anniversary of the Normandy landings was being commemorated over in France. Thousands of American veterans joined their Allied and German counterparts for a solemn tribute and reunion tours of the battlefields where they had fought decades earlier. Many of these men would have now been just hitting their stride in retirement. It was also the first time in nearly 40 years that many would be back together to ruminate on their reawakening past. And here it was that I woke up and was moved.

I returned to my high school alma mater in 1987 as a teacher of history. I found myself spending a good chunk of time each spring lecturing enthusiastically about World War II, and it was contagious. There was a palpable buzz in the classroom. All the students would raise a hand when I would call out for examples of grandparents or other relatives who had served in the war—frequently two hands would go up in the air. Every kid had a personal connection to the most cataclysmic event in the history of mankind—and in the late eighties, many of the soldiers, airmen, Marines, and sailors who came home from the war were still with us.

A few years later my students and I watched as the nation observed the 50th anniversary of the Pearl Harbor attack. After that we had the 50th anniversary of the Normandy landings, which again attracted much interest. The films *Schindler's List* and *Saving Private Ryan* were released to much fanfare and critical acclaim. The United States Holocaust Memorial Museum, a work in progress for over a decade, opened its doors on a cold April day in 1993. These events signaled to those who had lived through World War II that it was okay to begin to talk about these things, that maybe people were finally ready to listen.

Building on that blossoming interest, I created a simple survey for students to interview family members. I had hit upon something that every teacher searches for—a tool to motivate and encourage students to want to learn more, for the sake of just learning it.

I was haunted, though, by one survey that was returned. When asked to respond to a simple question, a shaky hand wrote back in all capitals:

I DON'T KNOW HOW YOU COULD MAKE YOUNG PEOPLE TO-DAY UNDERSTAND WHAT IT WAS LIKE TO GO THROUGH A NIGHTMARE LIKE WORLD WAR II.

He was right—nobody can interpret history like those who were there. Maybe I took that as an unconscious push to bring the engagement into the students' lives even more personally. Every spring we produced themed seminars and veterans' forums, and at every step of the way students were actively involved. We began to conduct videotaped interviews, inviting veterans into the classroom, and I also conducted dozens of interviews on my own outside of school. It seemed that for every facet of the war, if we dug deep enough, we could find someone who had lived it and would be willing to share his or her story. Young people who despised school stopped me in the hall to voice appreciation after listening to the veterans. I learned a lot about World War II, but I also learned a lot about teaching.

Shortly after the 50th anniversary of the end of the war we initiated a dedicated project, and to date, young people have fanned out into the community and collected nearly 200 stories, forging bonds and bridging generational divides, bringing happiness and companionship to their elders. They became 'collectors of memory' and brought back much of what you will read here, improving their 'people skills,' honing their capacity for sustained concentration and analytics, and sharpening their writing chops for college in the process. Just as importantly, students of history had a hand in creating new history, adding an important tack on the scholarship of World War II that would have probably otherwise been lost. In that regard, the books in this series are unlike other World War II titles on the bookshelves today.

Hardwired to History

Another early inspiration for this book is contextualized by an interview I did many years ago with Judge John A. Leary, a former Navy torpedo bomber pilot who later would go on to a distinguished legal career. Here was the young man who rubbed elbows with the likes of Joe Kennedy Jr., Pappy Boyington, Joe Foss, and others, the man who received the Navy Cross and the Silver Star for his actions in combat, but would not display the medals to the students at Hudson Falls High, instead showing me 'on the sly.'[3] Later Judge Leary invited me to his modest home, and I sat with him for hours on a warm spring Saturday night.

---

[3] Joe Kennedy Jr., older brother of the future president, was Leary's floor mate for a time while in training, and shared with his fellow Irishman a lust for life and his 'little black book' of female admirers. Kennedy was killed when his plane exploded on a voluntary mission over England in 1944. Gregory 'Pappy' Boyington and Joe Foss were 'larger than life' Marine Corps aces many times over in the Pacific and recipients of the Medal of Honor.

He settles into a comfortable chair across from me and lights up a cigarette, relaxing and clearly delighted with the company. His wife has passed, his children have long since moved on, and he and I are alone. With a twinkle in his eye, he tells me joke after joke and regales me with one incredible World War II story after the other. We laugh and pass the time; the lifeblood of this small town is being transfused as he recalls his life and his old companions in the quiet of his living room, and then he tells me something that will resonate with me to this day:

A little boy in the 1920s walks the streets of this town with his grandfather, hand in hand. They near the Soldiers Monument erected in the 1880s to remember the young men of the community who fell in the Civil War. The old man stops, points, and wipes his eye, proclaiming to the youngster that 'there stands nothing but a tribute to Southern marksmanship.'

Here is the young John Leary, who would go on to pilot dozens of harrowing combat missions in World War II, the little boy holding the hand of his aged grandfather, who had fought at terrible places like Gettysburg two generations earlier.

Soldiers Monument, Hudson Falls, on the Hudson River, in 1946.
Source: Hudson Falls High School Yearbook, 1946.

It is nearly midnight now, and it's time to leave. In shaking John Leary's hand I am suddenly conscious that I am now 'hardwired' to the past. An electric tingle goes up my spine; in my mind's eye I can see him flying as he steadies his torpedo bomber through a hail of anti-aircraft shrapnel exploding all around his plane, reciting his rosary prayers as he closes in to bomb the target. I am physically connected to the sixteen-year-old boy from our town who fought in the furious action at the turning point of the Civil War. I am just two persons removed from his fellow World War II veteran and later President of the United States, John F. Kennedy. In reaching out to other veterans, I am only one person away from FDR and Eisenhower, Chiang Kai-shek and Churchill; I'm just twice removed from the likes of Stalin and even Hitler!

A Higher Purpose

Still, as we recount these stories, the overarching question for some may be *'So what? Who cares?'*, and I suppose in our busy world that is to be expected. But somehow I believe that there is a higher purpose to this endeavor. There are always the lessons of sacrifice and service, of duty and honor, and that is enough to warrant a work like this. But in the end it comes down to simply listening, and pausing to consider all we have gone through together in a broader scope as a nation. It helps us to understand the essence of the eternal truths of the human condition, and ultimately, ourselves. World War II brought out the worst in humanity, but it also brought out the best. In studying World War II and the Holocaust, the ripples created generations ago remind us that history is not static, that these events will continue to flow and reverberate down through the ages.

John A. Leary, like most of the subjects for this book, has passed on. Thirty years after it all began, sometimes I will lie awake at night and wonder about it all. It appears that the past beckoned, and we channeled a portal. Here are the stories that a special generation of Americans told us for the future when we took the time to be still, and to listen.

Matthew Rozell
Washington County, New York
Memorial Day 2015

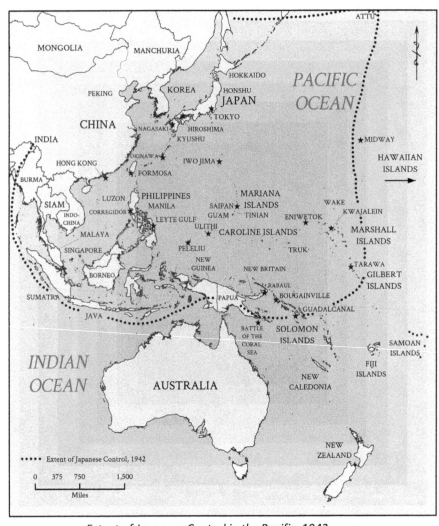

Extent of Japanese Control in the Pacific, 1942,
featuring battles and locations in the book.
Drafted by Susan Winchell,
after Donald L. Miller.

CHAPTER ONE

A Sunday Morning

On Saturday, December 6, 1941, life was good for the average high school student in America, despite the fact that war was raging in Europe and the Empire of Japan had begun its tenth year of conquest, massacre, slavery, and rape in Manchuria, Korea, and eastern China. While many families still struggled with the challenges brought by the Depression, most 'didn't know we were poor, because everyone seemed to be in the same situation.' Holiday preparations were underway and sports or other outdoor activities filled the time for most boys and girls outside of the classroom. Teenage romance bloomed, and football and basketball practice occupied many hours that fall. The Saturday matches were looked forward to all week, as interschool rivalries were fierce and led to especially-anticipated games between certain teams. Little did the players realize just how important their ability to function as a team unit would soon become—and for some, it would be a skill essential to their survival.

'Where the Heck is Pearl Harbor?'

The world changed on a dime that weekend when the Japanese Empire launched its early Sunday morning aerial attack on Pearl Harbor. In New York State, it was early afternoon. Church services had concluded; some families heard the announcement as they were traveling to relatives' homes for Sunday dinner. Many others were at home or in a car listening to the New York Giants football game on the radio. Some young people went bowling on Sunday afternoons, and others were in the local theaters to see the latest Abbott and Costello release when the show was interrupted and the announcement of the attack made. For the young people and their elders, the response was the same: outrage, followed by the universal question—'Where the heck is Pearl Harbor?' The other universal feeling was the uneasy realization that life was going to be significantly altered from here on out.

A few of the boys from the North Country surrounding the "Falls" were well acquainted with where the Pacific Fleet was anchored; they had joined the Navy already, and on December 7, 1941, they were onboard ship in Hawaii for the attack. At the time, over 180 ships and vessels were moored in the harbor. At 7:55 a.m., the first of two waves of Japanese planes struck.

Randy Holmes

A lanky kid from Hudson Falls was serving as a fire-control man on the *USS Oklahoma*, and that Sunday morning he may have been reading in his bunk, walking a duty shift, or maybe sidling through the chow line. With his parents' permission, Randy Holmes had left high school early, and had arrived at Pearl Harbor a few months before. Just 19, he was probably one of the youngest sailors out of nearly 1,900 crew members.

Dating from World War I, the 'Okie' was an older ship with thin armor plating, but had lately made a name for herself evacuating Americans trapped in Spain at the outbreak of the Spanish Civil War in 1936. Like many ships docked at Pearl Harbor that morning, she was in a state of complete unreadiness at the moment of the attack. Having returned to port following sea maneuvers only the day before, the ship had its anti-aircraft ammunition locked away and the normally closed watertight compartments below the waterline open in preparation for a fleet admiral's inspection the following Monday, the 8th.[1]

Barely minutes into the attack, as the airbases at Hickam and Wheeler Fields billowed smoke and flames and Battleship Row was coming under fire, the *Oklahoma* was struck by three Japanese torpedoes dropped at low altitude; crew members actually saw the torpedoes in the water with virtually no time to react.[2] The explosions ripped through the port side, with Randy and over 400 others trapped below her decks. The order was given to abandon ship, but as the ship listed and more torpedoes were taken into her port side, the men below deck were plunged into darkness as water flooded into the open compartments. In desperation, many tried to make it to the shell deck (from which it might be possible to reach the top of the ship and jump overboard) as oil from the damaged machines slickened the surfaces while the ship was rolling in the water. Dozens of 1,400-pound shells broke loose from their tiedowns; sailors screamed as the shells barreled towards them and they were crushed to death. When the ship took her fifth torpedo, she capsized completely around 8:08 a.m.

A frantic rescue operation by civilian shipyard crews with jack hammers and torches along the 'bottom' of the ship, now above water, over the next two days saved some 32 men, but it was beyond hope for most trapped below the waterline, where banging would be heard for several days.[4]

---

[4] During the salvage operations for the *West Virginia*, it was discovered that three men had survived for weeks in a watertight compartment, marking time on a calendar until two days before Christmas. Gregory, Eric. "Sixteen Days to Die...Families Weren't Told Of Sailors' Lingering Deaths." *Honolulu Advertiser*, Dec. 7, 1995.

The destruction of the *Oklahoma* had taken all of fifteen minutes, yet it would take Herculean efforts over the next eighteen months to recover the sailors' remains. Randy and over 400 others on the 'Okie' that morning would never return home.

Japanese view as the "Okie" is struck. U.S. Navy Archives.

The Japanese aircraft wheeled and dove in again. The *USS Arizona* suffered a direct hit with a nearly two-ton armor-piercing bomb, which penetrated below the main deck and ignited gunpowder in her forward ammunition magazine, instantly killing 1,177 crewmen.[3]

When the battle ended two hours later, over twenty ships had been sunk or damaged, including the *USS Utah*, which capsized with 50 men aboard.

Hailing from just a few miles to the north of Randy's hometown, Whitehall native Gerald 'Barney' Ross enlisted soon after an eventful career on the Railroaders' 1939 'undefeated, untied, and unscored upon' football team.

Gerald 'Barney' Ross

I was standing on the deck of the *USS Blue*, a destroyer. I had gotten up early that morning and was getting ready to go to church services. We were all alone out there at this buoy, tied up. I was waiting for a motor launch to pick me up and take me to a larger ship, where they had a chaplain; destroyers did not have chaplains because they were too small. I think that because the *Blue* was a small ship it probably saved my life, because the Japanese concentrated on those battleships. I was talking to a shipmate of mine waiting for the motor launch, and all at once I saw a plane go over our ship. I did not know what it was, but the fellow with me said, 'That's a Jap plane, Jesus!'[5] She went down and dropped a torpedo. Then I saw the *Utah* turn over.

I did not really know what to do. The searchlight was my battle station, but there was no need to be on a search light at 7:55 in the morning. Not only that, but two-thirds of the crew had been allowed to go to the shore because they had weekend passes. The only ones aboard were those who had the duty. I started to help bring the awnings down. When we were in Pearl like that, in order to get out of the sun, we always had awnings over the back end of the ship, the stern of the ship. We used to sit there on Sunday morning and read newspapers. Sunday was our day to relax...

Things were happening. So, anyway, while I'm out taking that down, the chief gunner, he's coming and running, trying to get into the magazine so we can get some ammunition going. We were caught flatfooted, everything was locked up... it was really a mess, you know, and we didn't have any kind of warning that the Japanese were coming.

He started breaking the locks on the ammunition. Everything was locked up for fear that someone might go in there with a cigarette or something. He said, 'Ross, follow me.' He took me down into the number three magazine. He said, 'I want you to take powder and shells, and send it up to the gun.' He showed me how to operate the hoist, and that's what I did. I'd get a shell—they weighed about 80 pounds, I think, but when I was 19 or 20 that was nothing, I could pick one of those up easy. So, that's what I did. I'd take a shell and then I'd take a bag of powder, I'd put it in the hoist, and then I would send it up to the gun.

In the meantime, we were getting under way. All we had aboard the ship that morning was one Annapolis graduate and three

---

[5] Mr. Robert Addison, one of our local Marines, explained for our young people: "When I am referring to our enemies as 'Japs,' for us, then, well, we called them 'Japs.' Nowadays, I refer to them as 'Japanese people.'"

reserves—all the top officers were ashore! We managed to get underway, and I don't know to this day why we didn't get struck or take a torpedo, but we didn't. We got outside of the exit of the harbor and we started dropping depth charges. There were Japanese submarines out there, and we got credit for two of them and credited for knocking down four planes on our way out. We were doing this with the *Phoenix* and the *St. Louis* and four or five other destroyers; our duty was to try and find the Japanese fleet. We formed up and started out.

We were out there searching for 36 hours. We never did find the Japanese fleet, and I am awfully glad that we didn't, because they had attacked us there with six carriers, three battleships, ten or fifteen cruisers, and about twenty destroyers. The planes alone would have taken care of us, so I was grateful that we never found them.

When we came back into Pearl, it was pitch dark, and we could see the fires from the *Arizona* and the other ships still burning in the harbor. They sent this commander out to bring us in because our young naval officer ... was not acquainted with coming into the harbor, especially because it was pitch dark. Anyway, it was a terrible mess, as you can imagine, these ships blowing apart... they destroyed the *Arizona*, hit the *Oklahoma* and tipped her over, and then the *Nevada*, she got hit, and the *California*, and the *Tennessee*, these are all big battleships; they sent about 300 planes in there, and it would have been like sitting here having 300 planes come and tear Hudson Falls apart. As a nation, we were sleeping; it is a terrible thing to say, but we just—I was just standing there waiting for a motor launch to take me to a bigger ship to go to Mass, to go to church! We had no inkling, no inkling whatsoever. We were sitting there like sitting ducks! Here are men, if you can visualize, men struggling to get out of the ships. A lot of them were sleeping in because they had the day off. It was a horrible thing! This fleet was coming to blow us off the face of the earth. [6]

Back in Glens Falls, Joseph P. Fiore was a seventeen–year-old soon-to-be Marine who would later go on to be wounded several times in action in combat against the Japanese in the Pacific.

Joe Fiore

I was on Warren Street in front of Lenny Bovac's news room. He had a table with all the newspapers on it out front and a big strap across it, with rocks on it holding it on the table, so they could put the extra that the *Post-Star* put out, and the headlines were, 'Japs Bomb Pearl Harbor!' So I looked at Ted Toomey and he looked at me, and I beat him to it—I said, 'Where the hell is Pearl Harbor?'

Well, not quite a year later I knew where Pearl Harbor was, because we came in on a ship, and when we entered the harbor—I'll never forget this—you couldn't hear *a thing*. The only thing you heard was the slush of the water as the boat was going in... And we saw all these ships leaning over on their sides, and so on, and so forth. So to answer the question, that's where I was, and ended up in Pearl Harbor.

---

[6] In his remembrances, Mr. Ross's voice began to break up recalling his friends who had passed before him. Barney brought smiles through the tears as he reminded the students that, "I may get emotional, but I'm still a tough guy." Barney passed away at the age of 94 in August 2015.

The Day of Infamy

Dan Orsini, 2011. Portrait by Robert H. Miller.

On December 8, the President of the United States asked Congress for a declaration of war. Dante 'Dan' Orsini had graduated from St. Mary's Academy in Glens Falls in 1939, and like so many others, decided to go into the service, as jobs were scarce at that time. By 1941, he was stationed in Washington, D.C., attending the Marine Corps Institute for specialized training; he was also assigned to a very special detail. At 21, he was the youngest sergeant-major in the Marine Corps.

Dan Orsini

I had only been in Washington, D.C. three months; already I'm a member of the White House Guard, which was quite a thing! The White House Guard is made up of sixty guys, each with week-long duties, and our job was to be near and protect the President of the

United States and go wherever he went, wherever the White House demanded that we go. So I had the opportunity to see many, many things that the normal person in life would not see.

I went to many events with the President on several occasions. I went to Warm Springs, Georgia, twice with his train; that was the Little White House in Georgia, that's where he died in 1945. I saw FDR swimming in his pool—nobody saw that; I knew that FDR was disabled, couldn't walk. He had polio. He had to be lifted out of his chair, he had to be wheel-chaired to wherever he went—you know, things like that. He was doing this for the exercise more than anything else, and his little dog was standing next to him, barking like hell... and that was very thrilling, seeing the President go by, saying, 'Hello, sergeant. How are you this morning?'...

On December 7 I was playing basketball at the U.S. naval facility in Washington, D.C. It was about one o'clock in the afternoon, and they stopped the ball game, and they said, 'We want you to know that we just found out that Pearl Harbor has been bombed.' So we finished our ball game [*laughs*] because we weren't sure how serious this was. We found out later.

When I got back to the barracks that night—this was still December the 7th—my name was on a bulletin board, and it said, 'You twenty will be at the House of Representatives tomorrow night; the President is going to address the nation.' That's when President Roosevelt gave his famous 'Day of Infamy' Speech. It still goes on record as one of the greatest speeches ever given by a President. He knew he had a job to do; he had to bring the country together to win the war. I was about 100, maybe 200 feet to him, right in the House of Representatives when he spoke. It was very inspiring, and he had everybody. He showed his leadership abilities then as President. Politics went out the window. He brought everybody together, and it's the same thing as saying, 'Hey, guys, we've got a war we've got to win. What are we going to do?' And from then on, the world changed. That's when America loaded its gun and decided, 'Hey, this is serious, the Japanese have attacked us, they destroyed our fleet.' It was a great victory for them; now it was our turn. We had to build our country up, and that's where we started.

On that tragic day at Pearl Harbor over 2,400 Americans were killed, with another 1,100 wounded. In the following hours the Japanese struck U.S. bases in the Philippines, Wake Island, and Guam, and also began attacks on Thailand, Malaya, and Hong Kong. On the 9th, Japan invaded the Gilbert Islands, and Germany and Italy declared war against the United States on the 11th. It was a shocking start to the war, whose prospects had loomed uneasily on every American's mind since the invasion of Poland two years earlier.

In the Philippines, the attack at Pearl Harbor came at 3:00 a.m. local time. Warren County natives John E. Parsons and Joseph G. Minder were with the U.S. Army's 803rd Engineer Aviation Battalion working on survey crews building runways to beef up military locations in the Philippines.

At Clark Field in the Philippines on Dec. 8, 1941, John Parsons was sitting on the steps of a barracks with some fellow soldiers watching an approaching flight of 56 planes, which a passing officer described as a "Navy formation." In a few minutes a thunderous crash of bombs began what would become a nightmare of horrors for Parsons and the other soldiers in the Philippines. Due to confusion at high levels and conflicting reports, the Japanese bombers achieved almost complete tactical surprise, knocking out half of the U.S. Far East Air Force on the ground.[4]

After entering the service in May 1941, twenty-four–year-old Joe Minder began to keep a diary. Little did he know the tortured story his completed narrative would reveal about his subsequent three and a half years as a prisoner of war at the hands of the Japanese Imperial Army. His entries for December 1941 highlight the confused nature of the start of America's war.

Joe Minder

O'Donnell Airfield

November 3, 1941

Arrived here at O'Donnell by truck. What a rough road and place for a camp—'cogon grass' [*kunai grass*] is higher than a man's head around here. There sure is going to be plenty of work building a camp here in this jungle! [*This would be turned into the horrific POW camp several months later.*]

December 7, 1941

Returned back to camp at 8:00 p.m. after spending the weekend on a pass at Baguio [*resort city to the north near the Lingayen Gulf*]. Traveled all over Baguio with Drake, a good buddy from Louisiana. Also went up on top of the mountain near a gold mine. That sure was a beautiful sight, going up the sharp, winding, zig-zag trail, cut in the side of those steep mountains. Had air raid practice at noon in Baguio.

December 8, 1941—9:00 a.m.

Paper just came in from Clark Field—*'Hawaii Bombed! War Declared!'*[7]

---

[7] Clark Field was the main U.S. airfield in the Philippines.

While we were eating... the first flight of Jap bombers went over our field to bomb Clark Field. Heard their explosions when the Japs dropped their bombs on oil dumps and ammunition dumps on Clark Field!

3:00 p.m.

Started tearing down tents, preparing to move all our equipment back into denser jungle to seek protection from Jap bombers.

7:00 p.m.

Just found out how much damage was done at Clark Field. Several hundred killed and injured. Much of the 803rd Engineers' equipment was destroyed; also several of our men were injured. Our surveying job broke up at noon. I have been put on a machine gun. So far, no Jap planes have come down close enough to get a shot at one.

December 9, 1941

Awakened early this morning by Jap observation plane. Thank God, no other planes came back to bomb or strafe us after he left. Just finished moving machine gun nest to the hill overlooking the airfield. Ready for action in case some of those high-flying bombers decide to come down and blow up our equipment on the field below us!

December 10 to December 22, 1941

For the past few days, hundreds of Jap planes have flown directly over our field on their way to bomb air fields, oil dumps, and ammunition dumps near here. So far, not a single plane has bothered us. We have been darn lucky! From this hill, I have seen many of the fires which they have set and heard the explosions of hundreds of tons of bombs. God only knows how many men were killed already.

December 23, 1941

Japs have broken through the lines and are now only a few miles from here. We are going to have to abandon this field and move to San Jose to construct an emergency landing field there. Things are getting hot!

December 25, 1941

Christmas Day! Sure doesn't feel like Christmas! Nothing different from any other day, except we were fortunate to have a little turkey for dinner. Sent a telegram home yesterday. Hope their Christmas at home isn't anything like this! Still on the machine gun here in San Jose.

Japanese infantry continued their steady advance from the north. The 803rd and other units, along with tens of thousands of Filipino troops, rushed to consolidated defensive positions on the mountainous Bataan Peninsula. At the tip of the peninsula at the entrance to Manila Bay lay the fortress island of Corregidor, where General MacArthur maintained his headquarters.

December 30, 1941

Japs broke through again! We are going to Orani [*on the Bataan Peninsula*] to work on another airfield.

December 31, 1941

We were bombed for the first time, as we were eating supper. Koltoff almost had his leg blown off and two other men from my company also were injured by shrapnel. Two large air corps gas trucks were also blown up, across the road from where we are. Several Filipinos were also killed. Twelve were buried alive when a bomb landed near their bomb shelter. Some of our men dug them out, but only two survived.

CHAPTER TWO

The Defenders

The degree of unpreparedness that faced the nation in the first months of the Pacific War was nearly overwhelming. Young Americans were hurled into a stratosphere of uncertain and unfolding events against battle-hardened Japanese forces. In the Philippines, a three-month death struggle would be waged as American and Filipino forces desperately tried to salvage their positions. Ordered to fall back to consolidate their lines, the defenders were confronted with the day-to-day realities of dealing with an enemy of superior numbers and experience.

By January 1942, the main island of Luzon was in the crosshairs of the Imperial Army and Navy, Japan now having a firm grip on all of Southeast Asia. After the fall of Manila on January 2, the Bataan Peninsula and the island of Corregidor were the only Allied holdouts in the region. The 803rd Engineer Aviation Battalion struggled valiantly to widen roads and repair airfields for the Allied reinforcements and counterattack that would never come. Fate would render her terrible hand to the 12,000 American troops and 65,000 Filipino defenders trapped here on Bataan. There would be no relief—only sickness and starvation, and tears of frustration and exhaustion.

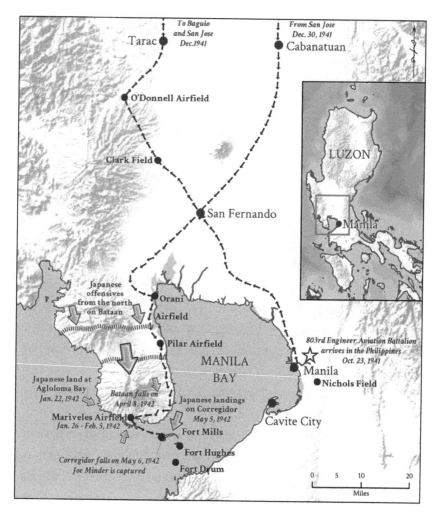

Route of Pvt. Joseph G. Minder in the Philippines, Oct. 1941-May 1942.

Joseph Minder was a country boy at heart, growing up in the Adirondack Mountains of northern Warren County with his brothers and sisters and a genuine love for people and the beauty of the natural world that surrounded him. He spent his days after school hunting and fishing or skiing on the mountain near his home. Like so many other young adults right out of high school, Joe would be literally thrust to the front lines of an unfolding titanic struggle that would engulf the entire world.

Joseph Minder, 1941.
Courtesy Minder Family.

Joe Minder

January 1, 1942

Darn tired this morning. Greco and myself celebrated New Year's Eve last night drinking warm beer in what was left of Orani. Spent the five dollars my sister Josephine sent me.

11:00 a.m.

Japs bombed and strafed while we were working on the field. Got my first shots at a Jap plane when I emptied my rifle as it came in to strafe the field. Saw the Jap plane catch fire and explode when it hit the ground!

4:00 p.m.

Japs spotted our foxholes and dropped frag bombs and strafed the heck out of us. One bomb landed 10 feet from the foxhole that John Delemater was in, knocking loose dirt from the sides of the foxhole on us. Although many bombs landed very near to many men and the entire area was machine gunned heavily, not a single man was injured today.

January 2, 1942

Spent half the night blowing up dud bombs which the Japs dropped yesterday. Darn tired but will have to work like heck today, preparing to move again, to Bogani Road on Bataan. This will make the fourth airfield that I have worked on which they have captured.

Retreat to Bataan

January 3, 1942

Started working on Bataan roads today. Shreppel and two other men were injured when Japs bombed us again today as we were working, building a bridge bypass.

January 4, 1942

Things were too 'hot' yesterday, so we worked last night instead of today, to get away from the Jap bombings. Intended to sleep today but found out we are going to have to move to Kilometer No. 201. Japs have bombed all the bivouacs [*improvised temporary camps*] around us. If we stay here we will be next...

January 5 to January 20, 1942

Although the Japs have been keeping us in hot water, bombing and strafing roads, trucks, bridges, and bivouacs areas, we have managed to keep most of our machinery running, widening the roads and building bridges here on Bataan for these past 15 days.

January 21, 1942: 9:00 p.m.

Japs must have made a deeper drive into Bataan. Heavy guns can be heard much clearer tonight.

1:00 a.m.

A lot of machine gun fire coming from the beach about a half mile from here.

The Japanese had turned a landing on the west coast of the peninsula, and now were attempting to surround and isolate American and Filipino positions. The defenders fought on tenaciously and contained the Japanese breakout, protecting the further withdrawal of troops and tens of thousands of civilians. In the Battle of the Points, these sick and hungry men killed over 2,000 Japanese invaders.

January 22, 1942

Japs landed at Agloloma [Bay] behind the lines last night about a mile from here. We have been notified to move in there this morning and help other outfits who are already fighting them.

January 23, 1942: 9:00 a.m.

First food and water since 6:00 a.m. yesterday. Fought 26 hours straight, with only one casualty!

2:00 p.m.

Many Jap snipers were all around us. I almost got it when one spotted me and started firing at me before I had the chance to get my machine gun set up! It was thick with vines that we had to cut our way through with our bayonets.

We managed to keep pushing the Japs back toward the beach till about 5:00 p.m., at which time we ran into crossfire from Jap machine gun nests. Before we could fall back, they broke the line and killed or wounded half of us. Robert Ray and Kenny, two close buddies of mine, were the unfortunate ones. Thank God, they were both killed instantly and didn't have to suffer like some of the rest did. The Japs tried to cut the rest of us off, but we waited until dark and managed to sneak back through their lines.

January 24, 1942

Found out at about 3:00 p.m. that we were being relieved by the Filipino scouts. The handful of us who were left went to Signal Hill [*the reconstituted Army headquarters near the city of Mariveles on the southern tip of Bataan*] to reorganize.

January 26, 1942

Left Signal Hill for Little Baguio [*a bit further inland, to the engineer depot at Kilometer Marker 168.5*] where we joined with Company B, 803rd Engineers to work on the roads again.

January 28, 1942

Visited men in Little Baguio hospital who were injured in Agloloma. Cappel and Peterson both lost their legs.

Retreat to Corregidor

February 4, 1942

We were notified this morning that we are to move to Correg-idor tonight and construct another airfield there.

Corregidor was the fortified island at the opening to Manila Bay, about three miles off the tip of the peninsula. Dotted with bunkers and riddled with tunnels, it had nearly thirty heavy gun batteries and twice that amount of large cannons for the defense of the Philippines. Situated not unlike Gibraltar in Europe at the strait entering the Mediterranean, it was expected to be able to withstand any enemy attack.[5] The most formi-dable structure was the Malinta Tunnel, a fortified tunnel complex con-structed between the wars that would go on to house General MacArthur's command as well as a thousand-bed hospital.[6]

February 5, 1942

Arrived here about four this morning. Everyplace we go, the Japs seem to follow us. Corregidor was shelled, from Cavite [*seven miles away, the by-now abandoned U.S. naval base for the Philippines*] for the first time today. Several shells landed in our bivouac area, but no one was injured.

General MacArthur was ordered by President Roosevelt to leave the Philippines for Australia to compose its defense in mid-March, leaving General Wainwright in charge. British Malaya and Singapore had fallen rapidly with the capture of 15,000 Australian soldiers, and air attacks in Australia had already commenced, shocking the world. The Japanese were simultaneously consolidating positions in New Guinea and elsewhere for the possible invasion. Meanwhile, at Bataan and Corregidor, troops con-tinued to struggle to hold the Japanese onslaught at bay. Rations became nonexistent; many of the men were subsisting on small handfuls of plain boiled rice twice a day. Enemy pressure continued to build.

March 24, 1942

The Japs have been shelling Corregidor every day since we landed here, but we didn't lose any men until today. They caught us out on the field this afternoon and gave us a terrific bombing which lasted about a half hour. Karp and Harrington were killed and many others injured. Most of our equipment was blown up. I thought my number was up when I was bounced around in a foxhole by some large bombs which landed about a hundred feet from me! Large fires broke out, so we left for Malinta Tunnel to determine how many men were injured and killed in the bombing.

March 25, 1942

Most of the trees were blown down, so we moved what was left of our supplies to the other side of Corregidor, seeking a little better bivouac which isn't as conspicuous from the air.

March 27, 1942

Company Commander Captain Zebowski died in Malinta Hospital from shrapnel wounds, which he received March 24th.

March 28 to April 7, 1942

Bombing and shelling of Corregidor is getting heavier every day. Japs are only a short distance from Mariveles. Heavy gun fire and gun flashes can be heard and seen across the bay at night.

April 8, 1942

Bataan fell! Men arrived here this morning who managed to get away by small boats and gave us the dope about what happened when the Japs succeeded in breaking the lines on Bataan!

The Bataan Death March

On April 8, the Japanese closed on weakened American lines on the Bataan Peninsula. By this point, most of the defenders were incapacitated by malaria, dysentery, fatigue, and starvation. Major General Edward P. King, Jr., commander of the ground forces on Bataan, received assurances that his men would be treated decently.[8] Glens Falls residents Robert B. Blakeslee and John Parsons were two of 78,000 taken prisoner on Bataan in the largest surrender by the United States Army in its history. Many men scrambled to make it across to Corregidor, where Joe was, but by this point for most it was too late.[7]

During the Bataan Death March, American and Filipino prisoners were forced to march in blazing heat for sixty-plus miles. Many stragglers were clubbed, shot, stabbed, bayoneted, or beheaded for sport and left where they lay; some Americans were even forced to bury alive their sick buddies who had fallen near the ditches on the side of the road. No accurate measure is possible, but perhaps 750 Americans and 5,000 Filipino prisoners died along the route. Barely able to stand near the end, the survivors were

---

[8] This assurance, of course, was immediately broken. One survivor recalled, "Mile after mile the looting and the beatings continued. They cared not who they struck. High ranking officers were no exception. I watched one private attack Major General King. The soldier was so short he had to jump to strike the general in the face with his fist. He did it time and time again, and the general just stood there...Guards with pointed rifles waited for us to do something. Finally, the private gave up in disgust and walked away." Machi, Mario, *Under the Rising Sun: Memories of a Japanese Prisoner of War.* Miranda, CA: Wolfenden Publishing, 1994. 70.

forced to double-time trot to the city of San Fernando, where they were crowded into boxcars for a five-hour rail journey. They were then forced to walk again for the last several miles to the notorious Camp O'Donnell, where over 16,000 more prisoners would die over the next two months.[8]

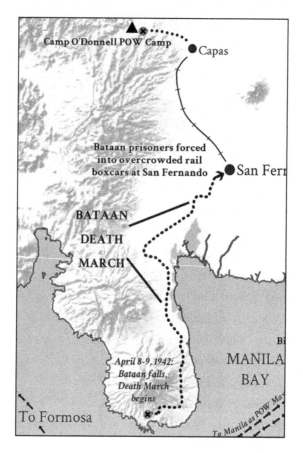

Route of Bataan Death March.

John Parsons' account was published after the war in the local newspaper.

"Of the 'Death March' Parsons says, 'It just can't be imagined.' The march was a distance of about 75 miles [*sic*], which was covered in around six days. For healthy troops that would not be exceptional, but for the sick and weak, as nearly all were, it was a cruel ordeal. It was not a continuous march, parade fashion, but rather continued over a period of about a week with groups of 500 being sent out each day. Parsons says they were forbidden to help anyone in any manner, even if he fell. To do so was to invite a rifle butt in the back. He saw three men bayoneted in the back at a rest period when they walked a few feet from their group and knelt over a puddle splashing water on their faces.

The Japanese way of feeding the prisoners, on those days when they did, was to place a bag of about 150 pounds of cooked rice at the head of the column and let them scramble for it. Those at the rear usually got nothing. More food was always promised 'tomorrow.' "9

In 2006, Death March survivor Major Richard M. Gordon gave an interview.

Richard M. Gordon

Words cannot really describe those days or the thousands of individual horrors. Suffice it to say, I went nine days without food and with very little water. My training as an infantryman paid off. I conserved water in my canteen by taking a sip, swishing it around in my mouth, and letting a little drip down my throat. I would do this until I reached the next potable water spot. Others, untrained and dying for water, would prostrate themselves along the side of the road and drink water from puddles. All this water was contaminated with flies and fly feces and brought on death from dysentery. Thousands of Filipinos and several hundred Americans died this way. The Japanese beat any who attempted to break ranks and obtain water, killing a number of them in the process. Japanese tanks, moving south to take up positions to attack Corregidor as we marched north, would deliberately drive over the dead and dying on the side of the road.

The Japanese were in a hurry to move in their reinforcements and artillery to pound Corregidor into submission before the final invasion. Before the march, Parsons and other prisoners were forced to excavate gun emplacements for the heavy weapons.

Joe Minder

Corregidor, April 9, 1942: 3:00 p.m.

The Japs have massed much artillery along the beaches facing Corregidor and are really giving us heck now. With only four miles of water between us and the mouth of their big guns, Corregidor is trembling as if there were an earthquake as these Jap shells tear into her sides, blowing up gun batteries, ammunition dumps, and setting large fires!

4:00 p.m.

Several boats were sunk trying to move around to the other side of Corregidor. "How long can this last, and why doesn't Corregidor fire back and quiet some of those Jap guns?" is the question in everyone's mind here.

April 10, 1942: 8:00 a.m.

Japs started their heavy bombardment early again this morning. Just found out that there are several hundred Americans concentrated in the vicinity of those Jap guns. That is the reason why Corregidor isn't firing back.

April 11, 1942

Corregidor is finally firing some of her guns in an attempt to cut down some of the intense Jap fire.[9]

4:00 p.m.

What an explosion! Japs just blew up several tons of black powder and TNT on Cavalry Point where we were bivouacked two weeks ago! Buildings, trees, and everything within a 500-yard radius were leveled to the ground!

April 12, 1942

Almost got it this morning, when I awakened to find shells dropping all around me. One of our trucks was blown up a few yards from where I slept!

April 13, 1942

Several more large buildings burned this morning by Jap shells. Our guns, which are firing at Japs, don't seem to be doing any good. For every shell which we send at them, about a hundred bounce back, cutting off telephones, roads, and all our communications here on Corregidor.

April 14 to April 30, 1942

In the past 16 days of constant shelling and bombing, the Japs have succeeded in burning about 3/4ths of the buildings and have blown up about half the gun batteries here. Dead tired! Haven't gotten hardly any sleep these past 16 days—night shelling and

---

[9] Many of Corregidor's big guns were made at the Watervliet Arsenal on the Hudson River, just a few miles to the south of the "Hometown, USA" region Mr. Minder hailed from. It has been in continuous operation since 1813.

bombings getting worse each night. We no sooner get asleep when we have to dive for a foxhole or a bomb-proof shelter! How much longer can we stand up under this terrific bombardment? Sent letter home by submarine the other day.

Soon the American gun batteries on small neighboring islands were also targeted, and they responded.

Corregidor and island forts.

May 1, 1942

Japs have lightened their fire on Corregidor a little and have started pounding Fort Hughes with heavy shelling and bombings. Fort Drum has started firing her 14-inch guns in a desperate attempt to blow up some of those hundreds of guns. Dirt and smoke rise many feet into the air as those huge shells from Fort Drum explode among the Jap guns! Corregidor is located between the Japs and Fort Drum and Fort Hughes, so we can get a bird's-eye view of the exchange of fire by the Japs and the other two forts.

May 2, 1942: 5:00 p.m.

Fort Hughes is taking a terrible pounding, in the vicinity of her large mortars, by Jap artillery. God! What explosions on both sides of us! Fort Drum is loping her 14-inch shells over Corregidor to Bataan, the Japs are sending all types of artillery shells over our heads to Fort Drum, and Fort Hughes is sending her large shells over our heads, also, to repay some of the steel that the Japs are so generously sending them. Some of those shells sound like freight trains passing overhead! With all these large shells passing directly over us, it makes our blood run cold, wondering if some of them might hit a tree, or fall short of their mark. Some of them sound close enough to touch as they go roaring over our head!

May 3, 1942

Worked late last night repairing roads, between the numerous shelling. Two more 803rd Engineer men killed by shells today.

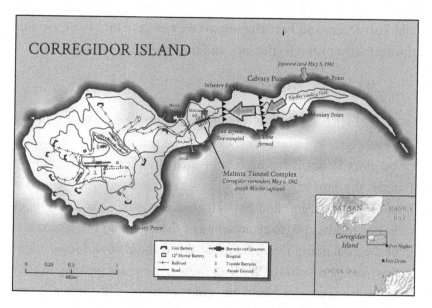

Japanese Invasion of Corregidor, May 1942.

May 4, 1942: 5:00 p.m.

Just saw the last two interisland boats sink, as the Japs scored several bomb hits by dive bombers, sinking them between here and Fort Hughes.

7:00 p.m.

Just finished helping putout fires started by Jap shelling. My clothes were blown up by a Jap shell!

Joseph Minder was turning 25 years old.

May 5, 1942

Plenty of fireworks to celebrate my birthday today! The Japs have been shelling and bombing continually since early this morning. All communications have been cut off from the other end of Corregidor!

5:00 p.m.

The Japs seem to be pounding this end of the island heavier than ever before. Marines were forced to leave the beach from their foxholes by Jap artillery.

The 4ᵗʰ Marine Regiment would shortly return to their positions to fight valiantly to try to turn back the invasion, claiming many Japanese lives, but at this point the enemy now had 75 big guns firing away at what amounted to point-blank range. [10]

11:00 p.m.

For the past three hours, there hasn't been a single break in the hundreds of shells which hit this end of the island!

11:30 p.m.

INVASION!

A runner just made his way over here through heavy artillery fire. JAPS HAVE LANDED, under this heavy artillery fire at Monkey Point, about an hour ago! The communications having been cut off, no one knew they had landed, only the men in the immediate vicinity of the invasion points!

A bunch of us loaded into a truck, which had all tires flat from shell shrapnel, and made our way over a shell-blasted road to site a machine gun on a small hill overlooking the beach and the airfield, only about 500 yards away, which the Japs had already succeeded in advancing to. We managed to hold the Japs at this point, except for the few Jap snipers who managed to filter through the gaps in our lines.

Artillery continued to blast away all night from Bataan and there was a fierce exchange of machine gun fire between us, but our losses were small during the night, as compared with large numbers of Japs which we killed while they attempted to mass-attack us. One of my biggest scares of the night was when an American mistook me for a Jap sniper, as I was moving up nearer to the Jap lines, and opened up with a tommy gun on me!

May 6, 1942: 5:00 a.m.

At first I thought I would be glad to see daylight, so we could see what we were doing, but when Jap planes started their daylight bombing and spotting for the artillery from Bataan, I soon changed my mind! With the cover of darkness gone, it was impossible for us to fire without being seen by the hundreds of snipers who had by this time stationed themselves all over the island!

8:00 a.m.

By this time we have suffered many losses; we managed, however, to continue holding back the main force of Japs until they started landing tanks. With no guns left to combat the tanks, we were forced to surrender at noon. Then is when I received the bad news of Drake's and Bailey's deaths, two very close buddies of mine. The last time that I saw Bailey was about midnight when he and I were firing at a Jap sniper from the same bomb crater. Dead tired, sweaty, and dirty with minor scratches and bruises suffered from diving in shell holes and going through the bush, I climbed on top of a stack of empty ammunition boxes and slept until 5 o'clock, at which time the Japs came and stripped us of most of our belongings and marched us down near the Malinta Tunnel, where we stayed for the night.

The Fall of Corregidor

The landing of the tanks finally decided the issue as they began to move up toward the Tunnel. With no possibility of relief and no good options, General Jonathan Wainwright radioed President Roosevelt, 'There is a limit of human endurance, and that point has long been passed.' The formal surrender on May 6 marked the fall of the Philippines. Like Joe, nearly 11,000 of the garrison on the 'Rock,' including 77 nurses, would now be at the mercy of their enemy.

May 7, 1942

[Forced to] work on airfield for Japs. Hot as heck!

May 8, 1942

Forced by Japs to bury American dead. God! What sights! Some were lying in foxholes bloated up twice their natural size! Buried one who had his hands tied to a tree with brutal marks all over his body, showing clearly what type of death he must have died when one of those cruel Japs got him. Some were torn up pretty bad, and after lying in the sun two or three days, the flies and smell from those poor boys' bodies was almost unbearable!

8:00 p.m.

Carried heavy load of Jap landing equipment on my back from the invasion point to top side of the island, about a three-mile hike. Thirsty as heck before I got there.

May 9, 1942

Sent to 92ⁿᵈ Garage [*an open-air, flat, ten-acre area on the south shore*] where about 1,200 prisoners were jammed into a very small space almost on top of one another. [11]

May 10 to May 22, 1942

With very little food and water and no sanitation at all around here, diseases started breaking out and the dead are beginning to pile up. Filth and flies around here are terrible! Dead bodies still lie on top of the hill uncovered, men who died on May 5/6. We tried to get permission to go up there and bury them, but they refused us. I guess those filthy Japs don't mind this terrible smell around here at all.

After days in the open sun, the Japanese began moving the men across the bay to Manila, parading the sick, wounded, and exhausted prisoners in a humiliating fashion down Dewey Boulevard on the way to their first prison.

May 23, 1942

Several thousand of us were packed into a small Jap freighter and landed at the end of Dewey Boulevard, south of Manila. From there we were marched through Manila to Bilibid Prison, a distance of about eight miles. Saw several men get kicked around by Japs because they were too weak to make the march.

6:00 p.m.

Received my first meal, prepared by the Japs, which consisted of plain rice. Slept outside on the ground until 5:00 a.m.

May 24, 1942

We were marched to the station, jammed into closed boxcars, a hundred men to a car, and sent to Cabanatuan [*what would become the largest American POW camp in the Far East*], where we stayed overnight in a schoolyard. [12]

May 25, 1942

Left Cabanatuan for Camp III, a distance of 12 miles. Several men were unable to carry their bags so were forced to throw them away. Others managed to drag themselves to camp but died from overexposure. I managed, however, to get through with a blanket and a few other odds and ends, suffering only from the lack of water and the intense heat of the day.

May 26 to June 15, 1942

Sick from diseases. Got very weak. Nothing but rice and thin onion soup since we arrived here. Saw four men get shot for trying to escape.

General MacArthur's Army of the Pacific had been defeated in less than half a year. Like most of the prisoners who survived, Joe Minder and John Parsons would spend three and a half years in captivity. For most of the men of the 803ʳᵈ Engineer Aviation Battalion, and all of the American captives of Bataan and Corregidor, eight months to a year would pass before family back home were properly notified. [13]

According to Major Gordon, General King told his men in an assembled prison camp session that 'we had been asked to "lay down a bunt to gain time." The baseball metaphor was probably the best way to explain [the "big picture" of the tragedy of Bataan and Corregidor].' The defense of Bataan thwarted Japanese timetables and planning, and forced them to commit many more troops than was expected, unsettling their ferocious drive in their conquest of the Pacific and, perhaps, Australia.

CHAPTER THREE

Captivity

The nightmare of being a prisoner of the Japanese Imperial Army was unfolding with a stunning rapidity. Joseph Minder continued to risk taking down notes and recording the horrors, never knowing if his diary would ever see the light of day. These actions must have helped to keep him going, especially when he could open himself to finding wonder and being thankful, even there.

Joe Minder

July 1 through July 3, 1942

Many men broke out with pellagra, beriberi, and scurvy, while others started losing their eyesight.[10] At this time the Japs decided to give us a little meat and mungo beans. I feel a lot better now but still darn weak. Weighed 115 pounds on July 4.

---

[10] Diseases brought on by vitamin deficiency. Various symptoms included fatigue, ulcerations, rapid weight loss, vomiting, vision irregularities, swelling, mental confusion, and lethargy.

August 1 to August 31, 1942

Still getting small amount of meat and beans but in too small amounts to do us much good. I started suffering from pellagra and scurvy along with others this past month. Many men still dying. Jay, Brozoski, and Nelson died recently. Three large details [*men who would be used as slave laborers*] left for Japan.

September 1 to September 30, 1942

Have regained a little strength back. Worked on latrine digging details and wood details outside of camp, also went to Cabanatuan once to load rice on trucks. Managed to get a little food from the Filipinos when I was on some wood details. Pretty risky business getting food from them, when our guards weren't looking, but we took those chances anyway.

October 1 to October 20, 1942

Had several hard rains in the past 20 days, making mud ankle-deep here. Japs have allowed us to have religious services but have placed certain restrictions on the way we worship, such as denying the chaplains the right to preach the gospels. I received communion on October 4 from Chaplain Brown.

October 28 to November 29, 1942

'Fifty Men to a Bucket of Rice'

Marched to Camp I at Cabanatuan, a distance of six miles, which is the main prison camp here in the Philippines. Food is scarcer now than anytime so far. Fifty men to a bucket of rice! The living conditions here are much worse than at Camp III. This camp is located in the center of huge rice paddies with swampland all around us.

The flies and mosquitoes are terrible. Two months ago they had a death rate which averaged 30 or more dying a day. Death rate has dropped somewhat, however we still have a death rate of 18 or more per day [out] of the 7,000 men who are packed here under these horrible conditions!

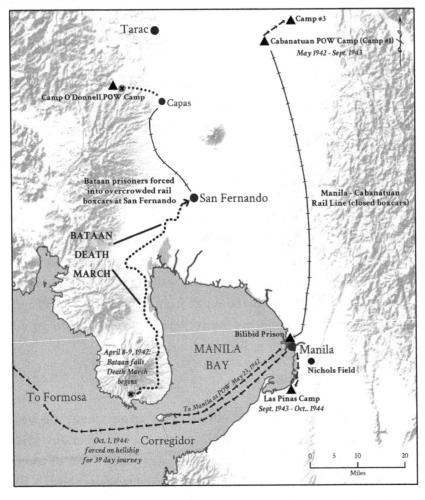

Prisoner of War Route of Pvt. Joseph G. Minder in the Philippines, May 1942-Oct 1944.

Chief Anderson and several other men from my company died. Volunteered for burial detail and have been carrying out men and burying them for the past two weeks at the rate of 15 per day. The first day was rather tough, but I don't mind it too bad now. The expression on some of their faces was horrifying at first, and not being embalmed, the smell was terrible, but I soon got used to it. Most of the men weigh less than 100 pounds when they die, but occasionally we run into one which is bloated up with beriberi and weighs twice his normal weight.

The cemetery that these boys are buried in and the improper conditions in which these darn Japs force us to bury those boys is horrible. Thank God, the mothers of these poor boys can't see any of these horrible sights.

November 30 to December 23, 1942

Things are beginning to look a little brighter around here now. The Japs have allowed the Filipinos to send us meat, mungo beans, and various other food items. Rainy season is nearly over so we go from one barracks to another without walking in ankle-deep mud. Above all, our death rate is about half from last month. My pellagra and scurvy is almost gone, but my eyes are very weak, due to certain vitamins which this diet lacks.

December 24, 1942

Attended Midnight Mass outdoors. Our arrangement was very simple, but this Mass was more impressive to me than any Midnight Mass before in my life. The altar was constructed of rough boards, the best we could get, and was covered in white sheets. Colored bottles were cut off, and candles placed in them—God only knows where they came from—served as lights for the altar. To make it more impressive and beautiful, it was an extremely clear night, with the moon and stars shining down on us as we prayed and worshipped there in our simple but heart-touching way. I'll never forget Christmas Eve 1942 as long as I live.

December 25, 1942

Christmas Day! Although we can't be home with our loved ones, we have plenty to be thankful for. This morning we all received a No. 10 package per man along with several other small gifts from the Philippine Red Cross. Much bulk food also came from the American Red Cross, which will be rationed out through the mess hall. But best of all, many new types of medicines came with the American Red Cross food. I know there were men today who offered prayers of thanks who probably never before in their life thought of thanking God for his wonderful blessings. This is the happiest day so far for most of us since the war began! Morale is sky-high around here tonight.

CHAPTER FOUR

Into the Fray

Back home, every morning brought more news. As the situation in the Philippines was deteriorating, the American public clamored for action. The President expressed his desire to the Joint Chiefs of Staff for a military response to Japan's attacks to boost public morale. Out of his wishes evolved the top-secret planning for the Doolittle Raid, where aircraft carrier-based planes would drop their bombs over Tokyo and Yokohama, and would attempt to crash land in China. The heavily modified B–25 bombers would be guided by a volunteer force of pilots who would train secretly before transferring to the West Coast to commence the operation. It was a deadly mission, as no one had attempted to fly a bomber off one of the early aircraft carriers.

Dorothy Schechter was a young civilian worker who had a ringside seat to the secret preparations for this first offensive action against Japan, a raid now legendary for its audacity and daring. She was in charge of accounting on various Army Air Corps bases for goods brought onto base to be sold to military personnel. At one base in South Carolina in early 1942, she was the only woman authorized to be on the premises, which made for some interesting moments.

Dorothy Schechter

When I got there I was the first woman on the base. They had no other women and they put me in a tent [*laughs*]. And one of the strange things about being the only woman on the base is the fact that there is no latrine for women on a base! And they suggested that I use the men's latrine, but call the military police each time I had to use it, so you can imagine what it was like for me. I had to call them up and say 'I have to use the latrine'; they would come and everything. They had to have their military arms with them, and so that's what I had to do. They were all very nice about it. But then after about a month they decided they needed to do something more than that. And so they found me a desk in the administrative building, which was very near the hangar, and they also made an actual ladies' room for me!

While I was on the base there working, there were a lot of B–25s... I don't know if you know what they are. They are military bombers, small ones, twin-tailed. And I saw there were a lot of them and I had been told this base was a transitional base, from a one-motor to a two-motor plane, which was very dangerous. There were numerous crashes. We would be working and the lights would go out and we would know that there had been a crash.

Practicing for the Doolittle Raid

I did not know at that time that most of the B–25s were for Jimmy Doolittle's group that he was forming. Of course, my whole story, it's like a jigsaw puzzle. I knew what I experienced, and then during the years that followed I learned from books what the rest of the story was, so that I had to put it together. So what I am saying to you is the combination of the two. But I have material that proves that it's all part and parcel of a real story.

So the master, the first sergeant, called me up one day and said to come up to the hangar area, up on the catwalk—you know what that is? Well, you know what a hangar is? Huge, huge, big place where they repair the airplanes. And then up along around the inside is like a catwalk. You go up the metal steps, you can walk, and you can see through it, and he said to come up to meet him and not say anything. So I went up the back way and went up on the catwalk, and he put his finger to his mouth [makes 'shushing' gesture]... We looked down at a group of men and that was the first time I saw Jimmy Doolittle...at that time he was going to several B–25 bases, gathering men, the best of the B–25 pilots, for the eventual raid over Tokyo off of the aircraft carrier *Hornet*, and it was the first time they had ever done that, to have bombers actually take off from an aircraft carrier. And they were sent to Columbia Army Air Base, which is in South Carolina, where I was. All of them were there for a while.

I thought there were a lot of B–25s. I couldn't imagine that a small base like that would have so many of them, but even they did not know what they ... were going to be doing. They thought they were to be watching for submarines in the Atlantic. They were supposed to be doing this sort of thing, and they didn't know until they got on the *Hornet*, at sea, what the actual thing was about...

There was some crazy training going on. And, of course, I didn't know what it was about. But they were putting chalk across the runways, with a flag on either end. And they took me out and showed me one, and the pilots had to take off before they hit that chalk mark on the runway. But the soldiers were telling me the strange part of it was, as soon as the pilots knew they could do that, they moved the chalk line closer and closer to the start point.

Well, we had no idea what it was, but they were training them to take off from the aircraft carrier—and they did it, every single one of them. And then they made a book and a movie from the raid called *Thirty Seconds over Tokyo*.

*"Take off from the deck of the USS HORNET of an Army B–25
on its way to take part in first U.S. air raid on Japan."
National Archives.*

Launched on April 18, 1942, 600 miles from Tokyo, the sixteen-bomber raid did little physical damage, but it did bring the war home to Japan in a way never experienced before. In the United States, it was considered a success and garnered much attention at a time when America was still trying to come to grips with how exactly to stop the Japanese offensives.

Internment

Later in the war Dorothy was assigned to the West Coast, where she encountered many Japanese-Americans interned during the war.

Towards the end when my husband [*a lawyer in Army intelligence*] was shipped out to California, I followed and there I did the same job I did in all the other air bases. I had to go every morning to the satellite base, collect the money, and see that everything was provided for the soldiers. And the first few days, I didn't see anybody. But after a few days there were two ladies of Japanese descent who came to stand near where I drove my car up to the office. And they just were standing up like this and bowed, and I said, 'Good morning' and they said, 'Good morning.' They seemed happy that I was talking to them, and then I went on about my way.

But after a week or ten days there were more and more people coming to greet me with this bowing thing. And I thought, 'What's going on?' Finally one of the ladies spoke and said, 'Is there any possibility that you could buy something for us from the main base if we give you the money for it?' And I said, 'Of course! I'd be glad to do it.'

I did not know they were Japanese internees—I did later, and as it turned out, I was in the middle of it. And this is what I did for them all during the time I was there. And they were so appreciative of it, if you realize how much they lost... they had their businesses, their homes, everything was taken away from them, and they were sent into camps behind wire... And it wasn't only about 20 years ago that the United States made some attempt at remuneration, not too long ago. But they of course didn't get nearly as much as what they should have gotten.[11]

---

[11] It is not clear if the women of Japanese descent were actually interned at this instance. Nevertheless, the episode illustrates the mood of the times that targeted Japanese-Americans.

Miracle at Midway

At the same time the men and women at Corregidor were being forced to capitulate in the Philippines, the first major U.S. naval engagement against the Imperial Navy was shaping up at the Coral Sea in the South Pacific bordering New Guinea, the Solomon Islands, and New Caledonia on May 4-8, 1942. The Japanese, bent on making a landing at Port Moresby in their push for isolating and perhaps invading Australia, were surprised at sea by the carriers Lexington and Yorktown. This was the first sea battle in history where the opposing fleets never even caught sight of one another, separated by 175 miles of ocean as the carrier-based pilots inflicted all of the damage. Each side lost a carrier and had another heavily damaged, so in conventional wisdom the engagement was seen as a draw, but it highlighted the American ability to level the playing field against a more experienced and aggressive foe.

A month later the Japanese sent a strike force of over 150 vessels to attack the U.S. base in the Midway Islands, a thousand miles from Pearl Harbor. The plan was to lure the remnants of the U.S. Fleet at Pearl Harbor and annihilate it once and for all, eliminating the strategic threat of the United States in the Pacific. It was not to be; Navy cryptologists had broken the operational code of the Imperial Fleet, and the Japanese trap backfired. In an amazing show of daring, Admiral Nimitz ordered his heavily outnumbered fleet out of Pearl Harbor to try to surprise the Japanese. Despite incurring early and heavy losses, the 'miracle at Midway' allowed the United States to send Admiral Yamamoto's fleet limping back to Japan short four of the six aircraft carriers with which they had attacked Pearl Harbor six months previously. In addition to losing nearly 250 aircraft and over 3,000 men, the Japanese High Command placed wounded survivors in quarantine and kept them from their own families to contain news of this astonishing defeat.[14] Historian John Keegan called it "the most stunning and decisive blow in the history of naval warfare."[15]

John A. Leary, July 1943.
Courtesy Leary family.

John A. Leary was born in Hudson Falls in 1919, and finished high school in 1936. As a kid he was interested with events unfolding in Europe, and kept a scrapbook of world events that would later prove to be prescient in regard to what destiny had planned for him. Like many boys, he was fascinated by flight and the dashing aces of World War I, and in hanging around a local airfield, he got the feel for the canvas-covered biplanes of that age. The old hands took a liking to him, and John was taught the rudiments of flying at age twelve.

After high school, young John tried to enlist to fly, but his father put an end to that idea, for a time. Instead, he went to Syracuse University, and immediately upon graduation in June 1941 was accepted into the Naval Air Service. A year later, he was commissioned as a Navy pilot and mastered aircraft carrier take-offs and landings, first in the Aleutian Islands, sometimes flying by instruments due to the dense fog and darkness, calculating life and death mathematical readings in his head to get him back to the ship. In a 2001 seminar, he offered his perspective on these first major naval engagements in the Pacific.

John A. Leary

Midway was the turning point of the war. We had been at the Battle of the Coral Sea where we lost the carrier *USS Lexington*. The *Yorktown* was badly damaged, but anyway, the Japanese did not continue to invade New Guinea or Australia.

Days later, after Coral Sea, when we arrived at Pearl Harbor, we thought we were going home because the *Yorktown* was so badly damaged. But Admiral Nimitz had other ideas and he outranked most of us [*laughter from audience*]. They put on civilian workers to repair the damage, and when the *Yorktown* sailed 72 hours later, it had quite a few civilian workers still aboard repairing. They never mentioned their losses in the war.

The Yorktown was lost at Midway.

Yorktown was hit again at Midway and they did abandon ship, but she stayed afloat and looked like she could make it, so about 200 men went back on board and unfortunately they were still on it when it was taken down by a submarine. But the battle was won principally, I think, from our intelligence, because we outmaneuvered and outsmarted the Japanese... But with the help of God the battle was won by the American carrier pilots, and [those] on *Yorktown* went over and landed on *Enterprise*, some on *Hornet*. So we were holding our own, and later I ended up at Guadalcanal, not too long after the Marines landed.

CHAPTER FIVE

A Turning Point: Guadalcanal

In any war, an apt metaphor is that sometimes hands are forced to be played before all the cards have been dealt. So it would be at Guadalcanal, the six-month-long battle that pitted young Americans for the first time offensively on land against veteran Japanese troops who were being reinforced on an almost nightly basis. While military planners in Washington debated these Marines' fate, they would fight on tenuously to survive. Indeed, it would be the incredible actions of these men, against overwhelming odds in the vicious jungle fighting, that would simply force the establishment in Washington to take notice.

As the first months of 1942 unfolded, an all-out military offensive against the Japanese seemed simply out of the question. General Alexander Archer Vandegrift began pulling together his 1st Marine Division that spring, and advance elements were gathering in New Zealand. It was expected that the division would have an additional six months to prepare for amphibious landings and jungle fighting, and no American offensive action was planned until early 1943. However, in mid-June, following the victory at Midway, intelligence showed that the Japanese were constructing an air base in the Solomon Islands at Guadalcanal. If they finished it, the noose menacing Australia would be complete and the Allied counteroffensive would become very difficult to implement and sustain. An amphibious landing had to be implemented immediately, the scale of which had not been attempted since the Allied disaster during the World War I debacle at Gallipoli in 1915—and with much less time to plan. 'I could not believe it,' General Vandegrift later recalled of the plan[16].

Nevertheless, the Japanese advance had to be checked, and out of these desperate times came the First Marine Raider Battalion. Schooled by Marine veterans of Central America and China operations in the 1920s and 1930s, specially selected young men became a lightly armed, highly mobile commando unit that could conduct operations in the sub-equatorial jungle, the vanguard for larger troop landings to follow. Edson's Raiders, named after their highly respected colonel, 'Red Mike' Edson, would earn combat honors in eighteen weeks of violent engagements at Guadalcanal that are unparalleled in Marine Corps history. Twenty-four Navy ships would be named in honor of individual members of the battalion before the war was over.[17]

Remarkably, out of the 900 original Raiders trained in punishing conditions, two veterans who resided around the "Falls" were members of this elite group. Robert Addison, originally from Ohio, would later spend 29 years as the Athletic Director of Adirondack Community College (SUNY Adirondack). He had a personal 'bone to pick' with the Japanese—his 19th birthday was that day of the attack on Pearl Harbor.

Robert Addison

I was home celebrating my birthday with a few of my friends. It was a Sunday and my youngest sister had gone to the movies. She came back and she said they stopped the movie and said they bombed Pearl Harbor. So that's when I heard about it. So we turned on the radio—no television during those days—and that's about all you could hear.

A month after the war started, I joined the Marine Corps, January 7, 1942, and was sent down to Parris Island for boot camp. Prior to the war, boot camp had been thirteen weeks. But they had to get a division; they had parts of a division, so they had to get a division ready quickly, so they cut boot camp to six weeks.

By this time, so many recruits were signing up that boot camp had to be cut short and advance training taken somewhere else.

Boot camp to me was not much [*snaps his fingers*] because I found that playing high school football in Ohio was harder than boot camp was. You were supposed to spend two weeks of close-order drill, three weeks on the rifle range, and a week of extended-order drill. Well, when it came close to the time for us to go to the rifle range, there was not any room down there because we recruits were coming in at five hundred a day, so after our close-order drill they gave us the week of extended-order drill and put five hundred of us on a train and shipped us up to Quantico to fire at the rifle range. When I was just about ready to finish boot camp they were filling up and forming this 'Raider' battalion.

22 Miles with a Pack and a Rifle

Addison made the cut. When interviewed by a Marine captain, he was told that the Raiders would be the 'cream of the Marine Corps' but was also warned that their mission would be likely 'first in and last out.'[18] He was accepted and was assigned to a mortar squad in the fledgling Raiders. More training would follow. Some days they would march, fully equipped, dozens of miles in the day, only to turn around and re-navigate the same terrain in the dark, through swamps and across rivers.

When we got into the Raider Battalion, then we really got into the force. On a Saturday morning we would go on a 22-mile, full pack, forced march in the morning and then they gave us liberty in the afternoon...And Edson was known for getting people in good physical condition. He was the type of guy, you would follow him anyplace, because what he would do when we were on these forced marches, he would stop and watch everybody go by and he would 'walkie-talkie' to the head of the column, and they would hold up and he would start jogging past the men double-time up to the head of the column... When we came in at the barracks he would stand there and watch every man go by and give compliments to us, you know, 'good job, good job.' That's the type of leader he was. Every-body practically worshipped him. He was quite a leader.[12]

Born in 1919, the other original Raider, Gerry West, pointed out to his teenage interviewer that his birth was unusual because he was born in the 'hospital at Glens Falls, and not at home.' He grew up in Fort Ann and, like many youths during the Depression, decided to enlist in the Marine Corps following high school. He was already a Marine when he heard the news of Pearl Harbor.

Gerry West

I'll never forget it. I was sitting in a barracks in Quantico, Vir-ginia. I had the duty that weekend, and there were about ten of us there listening to the Washington Redskins football game which had just started; maybe five minutes they had been playing. It

---

[12] Merritt 'Red Mike' Edson was born just over the border from Washington County in Rutland, Vermont, in 1897. Retiring as a USMC Brigadier General, he returned to Vermont and became the first Commissioner of the Vermont State Police.

started at one o'clock, and something like 1:05 they broke in with the announcement saying that the Japanese had attacked Pearl Harbor. You heard so much about all these meetings [*Japanese delegation in Washington, D.C.*], but still you didn't expect something like that to happen. So I couldn't believe it really, to tell you the truth.

West would join the Raiders and under expert tutelage be the first in his battalion to qualify for specialty pay as an expert in mortars, demolition explosives, and as a machine gunner.

They came out with the $6.00 a month pay for the four guys that were gunners, and I was the first one in the battalion to get that six bucks. Well, when you're making $21.00 a month, you make six more dollars, that's a big raise... Later, I went from private to platoon sergeant in fourteen months in the Raiders.

The Raiders embarked on a cross-country train journey and were then carried across the vast South Pacific to Samoa for two weeks on reconverted World War I destroyers. Strenuous training would continue with night operations, punishing hikes in rugged mountain terrain, hot, muggy weather, frequent rain, and steep ridges with slippery trails. They practiced landings in inflatable rubber boats, survived on skimpy rations, and were sometimes pushed from five in the morning until ten or twelve at night. Judo and bayonet training, first aid, stalking, and demolition were all part of the schedule.[19]

The Landings

In order to secure Guadalcanal, the Raiders were assigned to take the neighboring island of Tulagi, where they would be up against the best of the Japanese combat forces, the rikusentai—the Japanese Special Naval

Landing Forces. Coming in on Higgins boats[13] in the morning hours of August 7, 1942, the Raiders clashed for three days in vicious fighting characterized by hitherto unknown cave bunkers, their enemies' deadly sniper actions, night fighting, and their willingness to fight to the death. Thirty-eight Raiders would die, but the 350-man Japanese garrison would be eliminated with only three prisoners taken. [20]

Robert Addison

We went ashore eight months after Pearl Harbor to the day. Our battalion was given the task to take the island of Tulagi, which was across the North Channel. And it was only a little island about half a mile wide, three miles long. Before the war, this was the island residence for the governor of the British Solomon Islands—a beautiful little island, great grounds, great fields, and big, almost mansions there. And this is where the Japanese were...

---

[13] Higgins boats, also known as Landing Craft, Vehicle, Personnel (LCVP), were flat-bottomed, self-propelled watercraft capable of ferrying 36 men to shore. Men generally entered the boat by climbing down a cargo net hung from the side of their troop transport; they exited by charging down the boat's bow ramp. [www.higginsmemorial.com/design.asp]

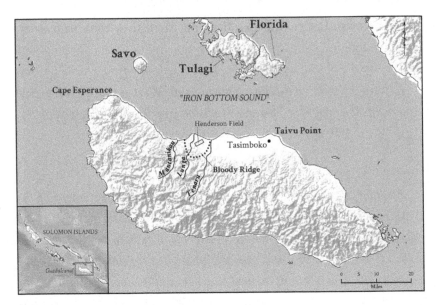

Guadalcanal, Sept. 1942.

On the first day, we had them in what we thought was a pocket... but, unbeknown to us, we had bypassed a lot of them who were in caves. And at night they came out, and then all hell broke loose in the night. They like to fight at night because they think it's a psychological thing. We think, 'Oh Jesus, they fight at night, they can see in the dark, they know what they're doing.' Well, it didn't take us long to figure out that they couldn't see any better than we could. So it took us a while to dig them out, and very few of them would surrender. We had darkened our faces. We had strips of burlap sacks painted green on our helmets, and after a few days what few Japs were left said, 'Don't let the men with the sacks on their heads get us!'

A lot of them we just left in the caves and blocked them up with explosives because they just wouldn't come out. And so it took us several more days to secure the island. Anyway, after we had taken

Tulagi, we kind of rested up a little bit, then they took us over to Guadalcanal.

Edson's Raiders, including Addison and West, were the very first Americans to engage the Japanese offensively on land in World War II.

'Confusion to the Extreme'

An hour after the Raiders landed on Tulagi, the other troops of the 1st Marine Division began to land unopposed at Guadalcanal, across the channel. Thomas Jones, another local Marine, was born in 1913, enlisted for his first tour in 1931, and rejoined later when the clouds of war began to form. His experience illustrated just how unprepared the nation was, and later, how chaotic the sea-to-land operations in the Guadalcanal campaign would be.

Tom Jones

When I was about to be drafted into the army, I decided against being drafted and reenlisted in the Marine Corps. Sometime late November or early December, we were called and sent to Parris Island ... on December 7 [1941], I recall we were standing waiting in line for our noonday meal, when we got the word, someone announced the Japs were now bombing Pearl Harbor. Of course that caused great excitement with us. From then on it was a lot of speculation and wondering what would happen next.

Late in May we went aboard trains and were taken to the west coast. We left San Francisco sometime during the first week in June. We landed in New Zealand late in June or early July; we were aboard ship for about 30 days. When we arrived in New Zealand, we disembarked and I remember it was during the rainy season. I believe it started to rain every day we were there and continued until we left, and what we did was unload our ship and reload an-other ship[14] to be transferred somewhere north of New Zealand. What island we didn't know, but before we left New Zealand, evidently the Joint Chiefs of Staff in Washington had gotten word that the Japanese were building up an island called Guadalcanal.

Things were confused, and when I say that, it was not the home-grown garden variety of confusion, but this was confusion to the extreme... We got to Guadalcanal, then we found out we had loaded our ammunition first and all our supplies on top of our ammunition! Now this was turning out to be a combat operation and we were going to make an assault on Guadalcanal, but fortunately, op-position was not that heavy... Part of the division [*the Raiders*] was landing across the bay at another island called Tulagi. Those Marines were hit pretty hard, casualties were relatively heavy in that battalion...Anyway, to get to the ammunition, we hauled all of this material that we had above the ammunition and we threw that over the side into the Pacific Ocean! That was part of the confusion.

The Japanese, who had never before experienced defeat, were taken by surprise by the audacity of the 1st Marine Division assaults, but immediately showed their skill at nighttime naval engagements. At the battle of Savo Island off the coast of Guadalcanal, the U.S. Navy suffered one of the worst defeats in history, losing four ships and over a thousand sailors during the night. When the men on the island surveyed the carnage the following day, the Navy was gone, taking with it most of the supplies and

---

[14] William Manchester clarifies: 'Wellington's [New Zealand] longshoremen chose this moment to go on strike. Drenched, sick Marines... had to load their own ships in eight-hour shifts, wrestling with soaked cardboard cartons which frequently burst open...because of the strike, they would have to at-tack with only ten days of ammunition and, in the words of a divisional or-der, other 'items actually required to live and fight.' Manchester, William. *Goodbye, Darkness: A Memoir of the Pacific War.* Boston: Little, Brown, 1987.167.

ammunition meant for the Marines on Guadalcanal. They would have to fend for themselves, and the 'Tokyo Express,' the destroyer convoys out of the Japanese stronghold at Rabaul, would be landing reinforcements nightly in the days and weeks to follow. Rabaul was the principal Japanese forward operating base in the South Pacific at New Guinea, with tens of thousands of troops in reserve.

The second part of the confusion was that a reconnaissance plane had picked up the Jap fleet headed toward us. Well, all the cargo ships got the word and left the area, but we left four cruisers behind and they didn't get the word about the Jap fleet coming down on them, so the night of August the 8th the Japs attacked our cruisers... consequently, we lost four cruisers. One of the cruisers, the *Astoria*, burnt. The next morning you looked out in the distance into the ocean and you could see the smoke. Eventually it sank.

Now we were on Guadalcanal. We had about three days' food supply in our packs, and all of our other stuff was gone. So we were now relying on Japanese supplies and equipment that we captured. Things were pretty tough for a while....

Jones was assigned to scout the Japanese.

Sometime after mid-August they sent me and Barney McCarthy and another guy out, Norbert Bush. Prior to our landing on the 'Canal,' the Japanese had landed in another spot, and it was logical that you should keep that spot in mind, because they might want to land there again sometime. So they sent us out—it was called a forward observation post. We concealed ourselves in the jungle. We arrived on the spot late in the afternoon, and no sooner than it got dark, we could see a couple of barges and they were starting to unload in that spot.

I was in charge of the post, so the next morning we kind of kept track of what we could see, and we could see they were unloading troops. And by morning the barges were gone, so I sent Bush back to report what we had seen and that left Barney McCarthy and me, and nothing happened during the day. We could look down and we could see the troops and what they were doing. Gee whiz, no sooner than it got dark again, the barges started showing up with more troops and supplies. Now I estimated there were so many troops, so I sent Barney back. Incidentally, all we had were three canteens of water and hardtack to eat.

Anyway, now Barney is gone, so it's now the third night, they are coming in again that night. And there are more troops, and I now estimated they had about 1,200 to 1,500. So I'm running out of water and hardtack, and I thought I'd better get in, so I left and went in and reported. Now that would be about the 16th or 17th of August—now I'm not sure of my dates, but anyway, we now knew... So we were expecting it [*a major attack, which came on the 21st*]. And they didn't disappoint us!

The Battle of the Tenaru

The first major attempt by the Japanese to retake Guadalcanal was to come at night. Nearly 900 battle-hardened frontline troops with over five years' fighting experience moved out silently toward Marine Corps lines.

Tom Jones

We had been able to string a single lane of barbed wire, Japanese barbed wire, we had captured. We were on one side of the Tenaru [*River, misnamed on Marine Corps maps, actually the Ilu River*], and they were coming from the other side, so they had to cross the Tenaru to get to us, and for some reason or another, I don't know,

the Japanese ... attacked on a narrow front; consequently, their casualties in wounded and dead were more or less bunched. They
would throw up a flare and you could see a target—boy, we laid
down a sheet of steel! During the night I think I fired off a hundred
rounds or better, and the rifle was an '03—it kicks like a mining
mule, it's a very accurate rifle.[15] The next morning I had a jaw on
me like I had the mumps, that damn rifle kicking me! Well, the next
morning we counted something like 600 dead Japs and we found
out it was the Ichiki Battalion; it was supposed to be the premier
fighting group of the Japanese, and it had had considerable success
in the Philippines and the Orient and they were hastily sent on to
Guadalcanal. And that was just the first battle.

*Jones was describing the first major Japanese offensive to regain con-
trol of Guadalcanal, where the enemy had 774 killed. The Marines lost 44
men. Still, night after night, the 'Tokyo Express' would continue to deliver
men and supplies to the island.*

Later, on another scouting patrol, he describes losing his best friend.

We were on patrol and this Jap, he shoots and he hits my buddy,
Barney McCarthy. The bullet hit him in the head and knocked his
helmet off. Now I'm looking around for the guy that shot. All of a
sudden he comes running out of the jungle and he's about from here
to the door from me [*motions*] and he doesn't see me. And he's grin-
ning from ear to ear. Then he spots me. I couldn't get the rifle to
my shoulder to aim, so I squeezed off the shot and I hit him in the

---

[15] Model 1903 Springfield Rifle, clip-loaded, 5-shot, bolt-action. It 'kicks like a
mule' because the 30.06 cartridge is very powerful. Used in WWI and WWII,
one WWI veteran recalled that U.S. troops in France could operate the '03
so rapidly and accurately that the Germans thought Americans had machine
guns. Army Times, www.armytimes.com/legacy/rar/1-292308-269297.php.

abdominal region; he jack-knifed and he went down. He threw his rifle. I immediately reloaded.

Rage is instantaneous. He's looking at me from a crawling position. I didn't shoot him; I went and kicked him in the head. Rage does funny things. After I kicked him, I shot and killed him.

By that time, the other guys in the platoon were coming. I took Barney's religious medals off his body and put them in his pocket.

You get so that you accept death. Anyway, I didn't think too much more about it until I got back to San Francisco. Then I remembered. Barney was from San Francisco. Barney's father worked for the Pacific Industrial Supply Company.

I'm walking around San Francisco and I see this building with 'Pacific Industrial Supply' on it. So I go in, to find his father. I asked the receptionist if they had a Mr. McCarthy. He owned it. I asked if I could see him. I told her to tell him I was Barney's friend and I was with him when he was killed. Mr. McCarthy came running out and that was the beginning of a real good friendship.[21]

Tom Jones saw much more action on the 'Canal.'

For the next four months it was very heavy fighting and battles at sea. Off the coast of Guadalcanal, the waterway there, they gave the name of the 'Iron Bottom Sound.' I think that fifty-some ships were sunk within a couple months there in these naval battles with the Japs. On a nightly basis we held no more than a mile of beachfront property, and we were consolidated in that area and the Japs would come down nightly with their cruisers and battleships and shell us. They'd get out of there before morning because we still had a few airplanes that could bomb them. That went on until sometime in October, when things began to change. The Japs would attack but we were able to beat them off.

Edson's Raiders Come Ashore

The Raiders were then assigned to be transported from the now-secured Tulagi to Guadalcanal following the Battle of the Tenaru.

Robert Addison

It was four or five o'clock in the afternoon when we got towards Guadalcanal. They were debating whether to have us stay on ship overnight or take us to shore. They decided to take us to shore. We had no sooner stepped on Guadalcanal, and the ship was gone! The Japs came over and bombed it, and in three minutes, it was down. That was one of the first close calls that we would remember.

The Raiders spent the next eighteen hours trying to rescue the oil-slicked survivors of the disaster. Six nights later two other transports were cut to pieces by Japanese destroyers, and the survivors deliberately run over and machine gunned in the water.[22] For the Marines on shore, such actions by the enemy would steel their hearts.

The First Raider Battalion was now tasked to the village of Tasimboko, where the Japanese reinforcements were landing. They also secured vital supplies and information about the intention of the Japanese to retake American-held positions.

Gerry West

We were there about eight days and they decided we'd make a raid on a place called Tasimboko, because the Japanese had been landing troops night after night. They would send a few hundred down on destroyers, land them, and get out of there before daylight.

The general [*Vandegrift*] kind of wanted to know what was going on, so that was the only way to find out. We made a landing early in the morning of September the 8th and found out that, yes, there was a considerable force at Tasimboko, which had already left there.

Robert Addison

Prior to our landing, the main force had moved back up into the jungles, and I think there were probably about 3,500 of them, and they left four pieces of artillery there which they were going to use on us when they attacked us. So we destroyed the artillery and pulled it out to sea. We blew up an ammunition dump, and we destroyed the food that we could not carry back with us. They had bicycles and everything there.

The Battle of Bloody Ridge

Gerry West

So the colonel [*Edson*] came back, and the next morning, he told the general the situation. He estimated there were three or four thousand troops there, and that's when we went up and manned this position, which turned out to be where the Battle of Bloody Ridge was three days later.

Most of the Japanese at Tasimboko had pulled back into the jungle. The Raiders took as much food and medicine as they could carry, and destroyed the rest, cutting open sacks of rice and fouling it with urine or gasoline. They also captured intelligence documents that showed a major action was planned to retake the airstrip that the Marines held, now dubbed Henderson Field. Colonel Edson convinced General Vandegrift to allow him to set up his Raiders on the ridge overlooking the airfield. The subsequent two-night Battle of Bloody Ridge would prove to be one of the most decisive of the six-month-long engagement.

Robert Addison

We got back into that perimeter defense. There was this spot on the longer ridge that was not covered, so that's where we were, because Colonel Edson had served in China before the war with contact with the Japanese military, so he knew the Japs—in fact, sometimes he knew what they were going to do before they did! He just knew that was where they were going to attack. Again they fought at night, and the first night they were scrimmaging, they were feeling us out and so forth... [And] the more we read and learn about this today, the scarier it gets. Poor Gerry, after our book came out,[16] he couldn't sleep for three nights because he found out that first night he was out on patrol, he didn't know it, but he was within a hundred yards or so of a whole battalion of Japanese! Fortunately they didn't meet, and about that same time I was out on an outpost that night. They didn't hit my outpost, but they did hit a couple others and overran them.

Gerry West

It's kind of hard to explain because you can't say you're scared then because there are too many things going on. You're probably more scared afterwards, when you think about all the things that happened, than you are right when it's happening.

---

[16] Alexander, Colonel Joseph H. *Edson's Raiders: The First Marine Raider Battalion in World War II.* Annapolis: Naval Institute Press, 2000. The definitive book on Edson's Raiders. Both Addison and West are profiled in it.

*One or two Raiders were captured, interrogated, and tortured with
blades during the first night. The whole battalion could hear their screams,
remembered one Marine²³. The Japanese would also taunt the Marines,
trying to get the Americans to reveal their positions.*

Well, anyway, the next day, Colonel Edson pulled us back a little
more, and the next night, they hit us in an onslaught! [17]Another
thing that helped protect us was the 11th Marines, which were artillery, and they were lobbing in 75s, 105s [*mm shells*], within 100
yards of us. If the Japanese had probed a little bit when they attacked
us that second night, they would have found that we had *nothing* on
our left flank, nothing. They could have probed and essentially surrounded us, and when I looked back the next morning, I thought
they had. But it was the 5th Marine Regiment who had been back
there waiting, and there they started to move up forward through
us.

Anyway, they did not get through us; if they had gotten through,
they would've had the airstrip back. The next morning, a Japanese
plane was so confident of victory that he came in to land, and you
can imagine the reception he got! Anyway, so we went through off
the ridge, and it became known now as 'Edson's Ridge,' or most of
us just refer to it as 'Bloody Ridge.' We had 50% casualties that
night, and we went back into the coconut grove [*the original base of
operations*].

---

[17] Edson to his officers: 'They [the Japanese] were testing. They'll be back. I
want all positions improved, all wire lines paralleled, a hot meal for the men.
Today dig, wire up tight, get some sleep. We'll all need it.' Edson and Raider
Major Ken Bailey would receive the Medal of Honor for their actions on the
Ridge. Manchester, William. *Goodbye, Darkness: A Memoir of the Pacific
War* (Boston: Little, Brown) 1987. p.189.

On September 14, 1942, first light revealed over a thousand Japanese dead on the ridge.[24] Outnumbered five to one, for two nights the Raiders held on against Japanese shelling by sea and Imperial troops, and the battle has become legendary in Marine Corps history.

Gerry West

It was probably the decisive battle of the whole campaign. In fact, history will record that without the Raider Battalion, we probably would not have held Guadalcanal. No question about it. I'm not saying that because I was in the Raider Battalion, but anyone who has studied Marine Corps history can attest to the fact that we saved the airfield those nights, because without it, it would have been another Bataan Death March. In the Battle of Bloody Ridge, just to give you an idea, two men in our battalion received the Congressional Medal of Honor and there were thirteen Navy Crosses awarded to men in our battalion just for that one battle, which is unheard of.

The Battle of the Matanikau River

The First Marine Raider Battalion would then be assigned to assist Lt. Col. Chesty Puller at the Battles of the Matanikau River, a jungle river about two hundred yards wide where it emptied into the bay near the airfield. It would change hands several times, and the fighting would be equally brutal. Nerves were also on edge. In total darkness, jungle noises, reptilian sounds, exotic birds screeching and calling to one another through the thick and rotting foliage increased the tension and terror— some of the men had been told that the Japanese signaled to each other imitating these sounds.

Gerry West

I think probably the strangest thing that happened to me was in the first Battle of the Matanikau River, I think about a week or ten days after Bloody Ridge when we went up the Matanikau for the first time. I was standing watch on a machine gun and it was raining when I heard a big thud. I thought of the Japanese; they [*snipers*] used to tie themselves in trees. I didn't know what it was, I heard this big thud. It really scared the heck out of me, and it was a big iguana about a foot long that had fallen out of this tree. He hit the ground and scampered off. He probably was as scared as I was!

They were on one side and we were on the other, but we were able to hold them off. We went out there a second time, on October 9 and 10, about three or four days before we left the island. In the second Battle of the Matanikau, we lost quite a few guys that night.

More than 700 Japanese were killed, and the Raiders drove the Japanese back into the jungle, suffering 200 of their own casualties.

Malaria

The Marines were exhausted. Rain was constant, bivouacs flooded, clothing rotted away. The air was hot, humid, fetid, and foul. Tropical insects and illnesses plagued the men.

Gerry West

One captain got sick, and then the next day another one got sick. By that time, we had lost quite a few to both dengue fever and malaria. They hadn't necessarily been evacuated from there; we got some of them back, but they were in sick bay, you know, to recover.

Tom Jones

Now one thing about Guadalcanal was malaria. Boy, we all got that! That is something. You get chills or a fever and you could be in the hot sun, the temperature well in the 100s, and you get those chills of malaria, your teeth are chattering and you're cold. I mean cold! And that lasts just so long and then you get a fever and you think you're going to boil over! It wasn't long after that they came out with a new drug called Atabrine, which was a preventive for malaria.[18] A mosquito carries malaria; if you had malaria in your blood and a mosquito goes in and siphons out a little of your blood and he goes and bites someone else, now he's transferred it to the next one. That's how it spreads.

By mid-November, the Navy in the South Pacific had re-grouped under Admiral Bull Halsey and won the significant naval Battle of Guadalcanal, enabling it to bring supplies and Army reinforcements to the island. Although it was suppressed from the public at the time, more than 7,000 U.S. Marines, soldiers, and sailors had died at Guadalcanal. Japanese losses were much higher. By the time the last starving and dispirited Japanese troops left in February 1943, further Japanese expansion into the South Pacific was halted.

Robert Addison

They called it Hell Island, the Japanese, because they had to live out in the jungles... They had lost over 26,000 men. A lot of them

---

[18] The "scuttlebutt" was that the new drug caused impotence, and it did cast the skin a pale yellow/orange. Some men refused to take it; finally, a corpsman would be assigned to the chow line to witness the men swallowing the tablet before meals.

died of starvation and diseases... When they left, they left 26,000 behind.

Bob Addison and Gerry West and the rest of the Raiders departed in October for New Caledonia for 'R & R', and to prepare for a vanguard assault on New Georgia in the Solomons. Tom Jones would be joined by thousands of fresh American troops, closing out a four-month stand of isolation. In the words of historian and Pacific veteran William Manchester, "There have been few such stands in history." Winston Churchill, in his later study of the battle, concluded with his assessment: "Long may the tale be told in the great Republic." [25] *Though the fight was far from over, and hard lessons were still to be learned, astounded Japanese strategists now thought that the situation was serious indeed: the Americans would fight.*

Gerry West and Robert Addison, 2011.
Portrait by Robert H. Miller.

Robert Addison

You know, the word 'Guadalcanal' to me is just like Hudson Falls, Glens Falls, Queensbury, and Fort Edward... [*He recites*]: 'Guadalcanal, Tulagi, Tasimboko, Matanikau, Enogai, Bairoko.' You know, engrained in me. I will never forget them—it's just like yesterday.[26]

*

Striking at the Serpent's Head

John A. Leary, the Navy pilot, was particularly fond of the Marines on the ground that he would protect, flying missions out of the newly secured Henderson Field for months and inching forward with the Marines on death-dealing raids under heavy fire.

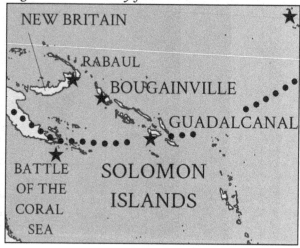

Solomon Islands Campaign.

John A. Leary

With one very short leave, we went from Guadalcanal and we ended up on Bougainville, so we covered the Solomon Islands [by air], all of them. And that cut the Japanese off because it destroyed their largest base at Rabaul Harbor, on New Britain. Rabaul had five Japanese airfields, a great harbor, and we could hit it from Bougainville, and we did.

Rabaul hosted hundreds of Japanese fighter planes and tens of thousands of troops. In November 1943, John Leary and his fellow pilots of squadron VC-38 [composed of fighters, dive bombers, and torpedo planes] commenced attacks in support of the Marine Corps landings below at Bougainville and hit supporting bases nearby. Bombing and strafing Japanese positions at Empress Augusta Bay on the 14th, 18 torpedo bomber fighters hit Imperial Japanese Army positions with pinpoint precision within 100 yards of the attacking Marines.

A radioman of his group recorded in his war diary: 'November 14, 1943—Attack Jap ground troops in the Empress Augusta Bay Region. Our ground troops had too much to handle so we dropped our hundred-pound bombs in their direction. We killed about 300 Japs and those who were still alive were stunned so that our troops just stuck them with a knife...[27]

Two nights later Leary was back in a night attack, sowing mines in the Buka Passage. For the next several weeks he and his radioman and gunner would be bombing and strafing Japanese positions in support of the ground campaign below. On December 13, he made a lone attack at heavy anti-aircraft positions on Puk Puk Island, scoring a direct hit with a 2000-pound bomb and successfully setting a radar building afire with his .50–caliber guns. At one point during his missions, Leary's plane was hit by anti-aircraft shrapnel, and a four-pound glowing shard lodged in his cockpit near his foot as he focused on guiding the plane back to base at Munda in New Georgia.

(L-R) Gunner L.E. Dale, Pilot John A. Leary,
Radioman Dale Greslie. Courtesy Leary family.

On February 17, 1944, Leary was part of a mission of two dozen tor-
pedo bombers to attack Japanese naval vessels near Rabaul. Diving in at
masthead level, Leary's plane scored a direct hit with a 2000-pound bomb
on a packed Japanese cargo ship.

John A. Leary

Those ships were reported by one of our submarines and they couldn't do anything about it because they had just finished up a patrol and were out of torpedoes. They followed these people with their naval escort into Rabaul Harbor. We were then called because we were the oldest outfit there. We were briefed, then set out somewhere around midnight. We hit them around dawn....I was probably about 55 or 70 feet above the ship...

Matthew Rozell: They could look up and see you if they wanted to. Were they firing at you pretty heavily?

Yes, they were, and it's rather difficult to fly when you have a rosary in each hand. I took more fellas in with me than I brought home that day, unfortunately. So the score wasn't 'twelve to nothing.' I was about 23 or 24. It was the principal Japanese airbase. They had five Japanese airfields defending it. They had about 200 to 250 Japanese fighters there, which could have been interesting. I was banged up a bit, but always made it back.

For his actions against Rabaul and elsewhere in the South Pacific, Leary was a recipient of the Silver Star and also the Navy Cross, second only to the Medal of Honor.[19]

---

[19] You can see Leary's flightlog, flight maps, and other bonus material at bit.ly/LearyGallery.

CHAPTER SIX

Sea Action

In 2003, I set out to interview a retiree living on the quiet boulevard leading up to our high school. I sat on his back porch with him for a few hours on a late spring afternoon. Born in 1922, he was in the Navy, serving as a radioman on a destroyer escort, and he seemed to be everywhere in the Pacific during World War II. Like John Leary, he also spent a great deal of time supporting the Marines, and saw his first action in the South Pacific in the reduction of the massive Japanese base at Rabaul on New Britain.

Alvin Peachman

I am from the coal-mining district of southwestern Pennsylvania, from a remote rural setting. I grew up in the horse and buggy days. I do remember Herbert Hoover, and I think when I was very young, a little bit about President Coolidge, too. When I was a boy we had the Great Depression, in which things were very rough. So I do remember that.

Most people then spoke of World War I. My father and his brother and my two other uncles were there. They had gone to France, and they all spoke of the western front in World War I. My great-grandfather was in the Civil War, but I didn't ever meet him. But at that time, when I was a boy, they still had Civil War veterans who were alive. I have a book from my hometown that shows them marching, and then they went by wagon, parading when they got a bit older, and then finally a few of them were in a truck or car, and then there were not any of them left; they got too old.

I was educated at a small country schoolhouse with two rooms. And then I walked to high school, three miles each way. I graduated in a class of 50; it was a fairly big school. The discipline was quite exact. I found our teachers were quite efficient.

When I heard about Pearl Harbor, I was playing ping-pong. I had just come into New York City because I had to get work. I found work on merchant ships, really as a longshoreman. I was doing it for about a week and a half when the war started. And so it didn't last long until I enlisted.

Since I had worked on ships and got to meet people, I thought I might like to be on a ship. So I enlisted in the Navy in 1942. I thought they were having a pretty good fight in the Pacific, and I was ready to get into it at that time. I was just about 20, not quite, yes, I was just about 20. A year after I got out of high school.

I went to Great Lakes, Illinois, to the University of Chicago, where I got my training, and then they gave us a lot of tests there and they determined it would be better for me to be in radio. I wanted to go into gunnery. But they gave you aptitude tests and they determine what field you should go in. I wasn't enthused about anything connected with radio at the time, but I then went into radio school. They said that was the best place for me. And I stayed there about four months for learning, and one month for guard duty; it was a very well-operated school.

Naval training was very exact. You had to march to class. You had to stand at attention before you sat down. You had to do everything just right. You couldn't speak or talk to anyone marching. I learned to swim there. And you learned how to live with people both through boot camp and school.

The Vast Pacific

From there I was shipped to California. And I got there and was very disappointed because I landed in what they call an 'ACORRN' outfit. It meant aviation, communication, ordinance radio, radar, navigation. What it involved was to get us ready for land invasions. We then were trained by the Marine Corps for rifle range and bayonet. Just like Marines, we practiced a lot of landings off the California coast, and then we set sail for the island of New Caledonia, which is a great big French island off the coast of Australia.

You see, the Pacific Ocean is so large that it encompasses about one-third of the surface of the earth. It is an enormous ocean; I think the Pacific would have more water than all the land combined in the world. It's really big! I know my first trip was 6,500 miles from California to New Caledonia.

It took us about three weeks to get there, and I know we all bathed in salt water the whole time; it was very difficult to stand it because it was like a suit of armor on you. I did not like New Caledonia because the French people there were very indifferent. They were not welcoming hosts at all.

We were jungle trained there. One day, the *President Adams,* a big troop ship manned by the regular Navy, came in. We were slated to go into Guadalcanal with the 3rd Marine Division. And they were very well equipped at that time, very fine soldiers. So, we got into Guadalcanal, which at that time was pretty well over—the battle had started a couple of months before that. As a matter of fact, two boys I grew up with who were brothers were killed in Guadalcanal.

In Guadalcanal we got further training, and I got shipped away from the Marines and got traded into [supporting the landings for] the New Zealand infantry, because they were going to make the next invasion near Bougainville at the Treasury Islands, which

mainly consists of about two small islands, Mono [and Stirling].
They put us in the northern part of any land forces at that time, so
our contingent supported anyone on landing ships with the New
Zealand infantry division. They put on a big attack on those islands.
They handled themselves really well and I got to meet a lot of good
friends there. The New Zealanders were really fine soldiers, well
taken care of, and we had quite a fight. They killed about five and a
half Japs to one, until we secured it.[20]

We established a radio base and then they took the jungle. It was
a great big rainforest. Our Seabees ['CBs'-Construction Battalion]
came in and they took the rainforest down, and in a few weeks we
had an enormous airfield there on Stirling Island, which was flat. It
was not a very large island, probably about three and a half miles
long and maybe a mile or mile and a half wide, but enough for what
we wanted. The airfield was so large it could take two bombers at a
time. The object of all of this was to knock out all the bases in Rabaul. Rabaul is in New Britain and New Britain was off New
Guinea.

We were on constant aerial attack for quite a while. The Japanese at that time were very powerful. They had big airbases in Rabaul and they even controlled Bougainville. Now Bougainville was
just north of us, about 20 miles, which was invaded by the Marines
about, oh, maybe a week or two later [John Leary supported this invasion from the air—see previous chapter]. The island is about 90 or 100
miles long, maybe about 40 miles wide of rugged rainforest. They
only took a small part, about 12 square miles. There was a very

---

[20] In supporting the New Zealand troops, Mr. Peachman was participating
with them in their first amphibious landing since the World War I Allied disaster at the battle of Gallipoli against the Turks in 1915. So many men from
'Down Under' were lost that the anniversary of the battle is commemorated
each year in Australia and New Zealand as a memorial day. After the invasion, an airstrip was built on the smaller Stirling Island.

mountainous volcano, just a very rough country out there. The natives there were very 'third world.' They were Melanesians and black people, they were very fine-looking people. They loved us and we traded with them. They got along very well with us. Only men could trade because the women were owned by the men. Boys and men would come down—they were very good at dickering.

One day, a friend and I bought an outrigger canoe so we could go out in the bay when things got safer. We stayed there from, I think it was October [1943] until early summer. And things did get better there. We fell behind the lines, things got too tame for me there. And one day, a ship came in called the *USS Witter.* Some of our men were being transferred and the captain told me and my buddy we were going to have to leave. One of us would go to New Guinea to practice what we were doing [*landings*] in the Solomon Islands. And the other would go aboard the ship. So I wanted to go aboard the ship, I wanted to get some sea action—I'd had enough of this jungle. My buddy wanted it too. So the captain gave us a game and I beat him out on it, and I got aboard the ship.

Six weeks later I got a letter from him with two pictures. That night his orders were changed and he went to Australia instead. He'd had a beautiful time on the beaches of Australia; he had two girls behind him and a nice big bottle of beer! So I kicked my own behind—I was always 'volunteered,' but this time I volunteered myself!

The Destroyer Escort

The ship duty was a lot harder than I had anticipated. On a ship you only had four hours on duty at a time and eight off, as a rule. Every morning an hour before sunrise, you had an hour duty at 'general quarters,' which was 'ready for action'; same thing in the evening, an hour after the sun went down. That's the two most dangerous times to be aboard a ship because of the cast of the ship's shadow and the silhouette out in the water; you were most apt to be attacked at that time, especially by U-boats [*submarines*], however, I was on a ship that was very deadly to U-boats. The destroyer escort had wonderful gear on it for that time. We had a crew of about 325—not a big ship, thinly armored, but we had about 26 guns on there.

Four hours on [duty] and eight hours off didn't last too long because often we'd go a thousand, or up to two thousand miles into enemy waters. Then, you would have four on, four off. Now at four off, you relieved your buddy for meals—we'd call that 'chow'—general quarters, or anything at all. You weren't off at all. Now when they put stores aboard for your provisions or ammunition, all hands had to show forth. So, if they pulled into the place at midnight, you had to get out of bed and help load these groceries or these bullets and whatever else you had. It was a lot of work. You could not backslide on anything. You had a lot of responsibility. Therefore, I found it harder than being on land.

I had a commander whose name was "Fearless Freddy." He was a very unique character who a lot of people thought was psychologically off. He loved battle extremely and he expected you to be that way, too. He wanted you to be a red-blooded American. He loved battle more than any man I've ever met. I would rank him with General Custer or General Patton or someone. He wasn't afraid of the devil! He won a big medal in the beginning of the war on the *Lexington,* and I think he was aboard every one of our group of ships when they were hit in Okinawa! They said he jinxed everything. But he loved fighting.

Rescue

I think the first thing we did, after working around Bougainville and Emirau Island, [was a rescue operation]. We got a call one day to rescue a downed Marine plane near Truk in the Caroline Islands, one of the great Japanese forward bases. This Marine plane went up there and bombed it, and it was hit by anti-aircraft fire and fell at sea. Our mission was to go and rescue them, and we were about 1,500 miles away, so we went up into that region and made a search. We would go a couple square miles in each direction, in a box-like direction. And we had no results after three days because we got another call, there had been a big wind and the plane was seen about 200 miles to the west. So we steamed in that direction and again, we could not find them. After the fourth day we were told to leave, but our captain was a very fine gentleman, and he said he could not do that. He said, 'We'll cut our power to conserve our fuel and we'll keep looking.'

On the fifth day, at night, we thought we had a submarine scare and so we started to fire depth charges; I guess it made a great big flame at night, and way out in the far distance, we noticed a flare! So, we headed out and found these Marines! Two had been killed. I believe there were five of them and their faces were three times the size of normal. They were all in the water, except for the officer who was alive but injured, and all these guys were struggling with sharks! So, we put them aboard and they were very happy and we were happy, too. One of them had my bed, later. They told us they would never criticize the Navy! It took about three or four days to bring them back to base.

They were almost on the equator. I would say I crossed the equator sixty times, being on the *Witter*. Then we took part in the New Guinea operations. In New Guinea, like everywhere else in the war, we had the 'hop, skip, and jump' philosophy. And that meant you maybe took one island out of ten, and neutralized the rest by air and sea. In New Guinea we just hopped along the coast. Now New Guinea is a very large, mysterious, beautiful island. I had been all over the coast. And it would be about from here [*upstate New York*] to Denver, Colorado, in length, extremely big and that includes great big mountains that you can see from the shore and enormous rain forests, just tremendous amounts of rain. The rain we have here is nothing. You could get a few feet in the ground in no time! I know when we lived in the tents on that island we were always wet, extremely wet. They also had large meadows and big rivers and all kinds of natives, and some of them were very black and very different.

After that, we worked that whole region and we did a lot of convoy duty, and one day after a long period of time we were to go to Australia. That night, being the radioman [on duty] taking Morse code, I found out that our orders had been changed. I think that night our captain got drunk and insulted the 'big guy' on shore! The guys were up cleaning their gear the next day to go to Australia, and I said to them, 'You're not going anywhere,' and they said, 'Well, maybe instead we will go to Hawaii,' and I said, 'Well, you're not getting in there, either.' So we had to make this long journey, 5,500 miles to Hawaii, and when we got about a hundred miles from Hawaii, we were relieved of our convoy duties! And we were ordered [back] to the Marshall Islands... [In all] it was three weeks, an 11,000 mile trip![28]

As the book went to press, I was contacted by Japan's largest news wire service, "with over 50 million subscribers worldwide, publishing articles in Japanese, English, Chinese, and in Korean..." They wanted a veteran's "reflections as we approach the 70th anniversary of the double bombings of Hiroshima and Nagasaki" (which he offers in Chapter 13, 'The

Kamikazes'). So, seventy years after the war, Mr. Peachman got to address the Japanese people.

Alvin Peachman. Author photo.

Mr. Peachman was my high school U.S. history teacher. At the time, I had no idea that he had fought in World War II.

CHAPTER SEVEN

Captivity-Year 2

As 1943 unfolded, America entered its second year of war. In Europe, the Axis war machine was being confronted in North Africa and at Stalingrad. Vast amounts of men and materiel were being poured into the fight as Sicily and Italy loomed large as new Allied invasion targets, with the planning for the Normandy landings already commenced. Britain had staved off an invasion by Nazi Germany and by mid-year was resembling a floating air base as nearly a million GIs crowded encampments there to prepare for the great invasion of France.

In the Pacific, the Allies were also on the move in coordinated attacks, following up on the successes in the Solomons and elsewhere. But for prisoners of war like Joseph Minder with little concrete information, conclusions had to be teased out of scant information and the increasingly belligerent attitudes of their captors.

'Someone is Getting a Cruel Beating'

Joe Minder

January 21 to May 1, 1943

During these past four months, I have worked cutting wood, carrying hay, digging long draining ditches, planting and taking part in this useless garden, and made a few burial details. The Japs must be suffering heavy losses on their battlefronts, by the way they are treating us now. They have cut down our food again and have started beating the heck out of us, on various work details.

May 1, 1943

Every time we look around someone is getting a cruel beating for some darn thing. I got hit in the head by a bayonet, crushing my sun helmet and putting a lump on my head, which I carried for a week. My worries would be over now if that Jap would have hit me with the sharp edge of that bayonet!

May 2, 1943

Started building new garden across the road from the hospital.

May 3, 1943

Rainy season has started. The mud finished tearing up my old rotten shoes which I brought from Corregidor, so I'll have to go barefoot now.

May 4, 1943

Worked laying stone foundation for 'Burma Road,' as we called it. Several of us got the heck beat out of us for dropping large stones which were too heavy to handle as we passed them from one to another.

Joe's second year in captivity was beginning on his birthday.

May 5, 1943

Hope a year from today I am celebrating my birthday under the Yanks. I'll celebrate today by eating rice and greens soup!

May 6 to May 29, 1943

Food is constantly getting worse and these darn Formosan guards [*Japanese guards who previously had duty at the notorious island camps on Taiwan*], armed with clubs, are using them plenty every day. Saw a guy get a hose broken across his back yesterday! Two men escaped this week. So far they haven't been able to find them. That of course made things worse. After they escaped, the Japs doubled the guard and made it stricter than ever on us.

'Made to Dig Their Own Graves'

John Parsons, captured on Bataan in April 1942, described a new policy he witnessed in subsequent escape attempts.

John Parsons

Prisoners were put in groups of ten, a policy which was in effect from then on, and in the event any one man attempted to escape or made any move which might be construed as such, the other nine were put to death with him. When this did happen, the ten condemned were made to dig their own graves the afternoon prior to their deaths. Then four stakes were driven around the pit and the man was tied hand and foot spread-eagle over the hole so he was forced to stare at his own grave all night. In the morning the entire camp was turned out to witness the executions and the condemned were offered a cigarette and a blindfold, the latter of which was usually refused.[29]

'The Mothers Back Home'

Joe Minder

May 30, 1943

Japs allowed us to have memorial services for the 2,644 who have died since this camp opened, less than a year ago. About 2,100 of us attended the services. It made me shudder when I looked around at the huge crowd and remembered that there was even a larger amount than that piled on top of one another in this small, swampy half acre of ground. Only 11 months ago they were all with us, but their fear of the Japs' clubs is over now. I almost cried when I thought of the mothers back home who are waiting for their return.

May 31 to June 30, 1943

Several papers have been smuggled in from the Filipinos. We understand now why we are getting such rough treatment. Those 'Yanks' are kicking the heck out of them now! The Japs are also killing and burning down many Filipino villages now. Some Filipino guerrillas killed some Jap guards on a bridge near here and the Japs retaliated by dive bombing, and burnt the entire village.

July 1 to August 1, 1943

The Japs have enlarged this farm and are forcing the officers to work with us now. They are making everybody go barefoot now. The officers are having a heck of a time wading in this mud and walking over these sharp stones with their bare feet. I have been barefoot for three months, so my feet are pretty tough now.

August 2 to September 17, 1943

Even though we aren't getting hardly any meat or extra food from the outside, our morale is high in the sky. We found out through a paper smuggled in by a Filipino that the Yanks had landed in Italy!

This camp is much smaller now. Several hundred have been taken out to work on airfields in the Philippines, while others left for Japan. I was scheduled to go to Japan but my name was taken off. I'll be one of the first to go after the first bunch leaves here.

September 18, 1943

About 800 of us are packed and ready to leave camp to go work somewhere in the Philippines. No one knows where we are going.

12 Noon

We all made this hike of five miles pretty good and are now waiting here on trains to go towards Manila. These old shoes which I wired together are still staying on my feet. Didn't even get a blister out of that hike!

6:00 p.m.

Jap navy personnel met us here in Manila railroad station with trucks. Just found out that we are going to go to Las Pinas to work on an airfield.

7:00 p.m.

Raining hard. We arrived here to find out this camp is only another mudhole like the grounds at Camp I.

9:00 p.m.

Dead tired. I flopped down on the floor, 50 of us packed in a small room and I got a good night's sleep. This makes the fifth prison camp which I have been in since I have been taken prisoner.

September 20 to November 15, 1943

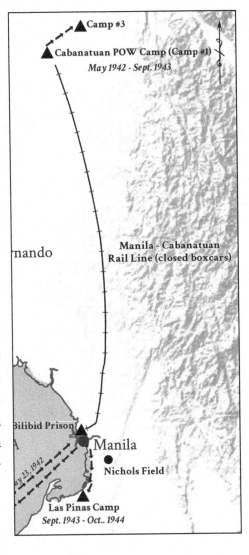

Things have been pretty good here for the past two months. In the middle of October, 150 new men came down from Camp I to replace the 150 men who had dysentery. My buddy, Greco, was one of the ones who had dysentery, so he went back to Camp I, also.

Working conditions aren't too bad. We have been levying down rice paddies. No one has received any beatings yet. This detail wouldn't be half so bad if we only had shoes to protect our feet.

Food is a lot of fish. Although it is rotten as heck we boiled it up and made fish soup using heads, guts, and even the bones. Some of the guys can't do it, but I force it down because I know there is a lot of protein in it. In fact, I'm not suffering from pellagra or scurvy anymore and my eyes don't bother me much now. We also received a little extra food from the Philippine Red Cross.

November 16 to November 23, 1943

Started working harder now, digging deep drainage ditches. They started using their clubs. I thought these guards wouldn't be so bad, but they are as rough as those Japs at Camp I. Frank Bollinger, myself, and about 50 others got beat across the back by a raging drunk supervisor about a week ago. I'm still carrying some of those club marks.

Three and a half thousand miles away in the south-central Pacific, unbeknownst to Joe and his fellow prisoners, an intense battle was winding down at a tiny coral atoll called Tarawa in the Gilbert Islands.

November 24, 1943

Not a bad Thanksgiving. Each one of us received a No. 10 food parcel from the American Red Cross. Those candy bars and the cheese and corned beef are wonderful. We stayed up until two this morning drinking coffee and eating. We will at least have our bellies full until we finish that final bit of American food.

November 25 to December 24, 1943

We have made connection with the Filipinos out at work and they are selling our American cigarettes on the black market in Manila and are giving us food and money for them. Hope none of us gets caught dealing with them. Japs have already said they would kill us if we got caught dealing with the Filipinos.

December 25, 1943

Christmas Day! Each of us received another food parcel. Also about half of us received American Red Cross GI shoes. I have gone without shoes so long now I doubt if I will have strength enough to carry those heavy shoes, especially through this deep, sticky mud.

CHAPTER EIGHT

Islands of the Damned

As 1943 turned into 1944, the objective turned to cutting off and destroying Japanese forward positions still operating in the South Pacific while also taking the Marshall and Mariana Islands in the Central Pacific, ratcheting up the pressure on the enemy in simultaneous operations. Coral Sea, Midway, and Guadalcanal had demonstrated America's grit and mettle, but the first test of a new type of amphibious landing operations for the coral islands was at the invasion at Tarawa Atoll in the Gilberts in November 1943. It was a three-day bloodletting and a brutal lesson for the American forces; over 1,000 Marines and nearly 700 sailors were killed in less than 80 hours, and Japanese dead numbered nearly 4,700, with only seventeen prisoners taken.

The island battles of 1944 set the stage for the major operations to follow in 1945. For the Japanese, it would be do-or-die. Entire garrisons were committed to fighting to the death in a tradition that celebrated suicide before surrender, condemning them and thousands of Americans to death.

Hailing originally from the Bronx, Ralph Leinoff was assigned to the 4th Marine Division as part of a machine gun squad.

Tarawa

Marines Under Fire, Tarawa, November 1943. USMC. Public domain.

Ralph Leinoff

Tarawa was an atoll island. I don't know if you're familiar with a map of the Pacific, but it consists of a lot of underground mountains, which really, above the water, become 'atolls,' tiny little islands. And the operation before us was Tarawa, and we took heavy losses on Tarawa, because we were using Higgins boats, which were not able to negotiate the coral reefs. We got hung up on the coral reefs, which meant that the men all had to get to shore; they had to wade through hundreds of yards of water to get through. It's very shallow water in the coral reefs. And of course the coral is very sharp. It would tear your shoes, and they were sitting ducks; there was no place to get cover. So we took an awful beating on Tarawa. At that time, then, it was decided that we have to do something else.

We can't use the Higgins boats—Higgins boats were good in that they were very, very fast. They moved right along. But we needed a tracked vehicle, like a tank that could float. And they invented the...the half-track, which was a true carrier, an open-top, true carrier, and that could ride right over the coral. If you got in it, it moved very slow; it didn't have propellers on it. The cleats on the treads, the tank treads, were the propulsion device. It would push the water back and the vehicle would go forward. And it held maybe about ten men or so, but it was very, very slow-moving, and we had casualties.

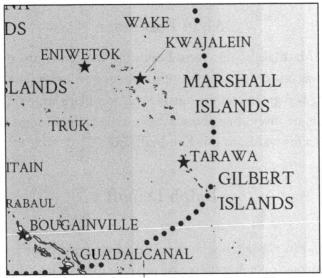

The Marshalls.

The Marshall Atolls

With its tiny airfield, Tarawa became a necessary stepping stone to the Marshall Island atoll group, and thence to the much larger islands in the Marianas, from where the sleek new B–29 bombers now rolling off the assembly lines at home would find the range to the cities of Japan. Here, in the Central Pacific, working in tandem with the burgeoning U.S. Navy under Admiral Nimitz, U.S. Marines and Navy flyers advanced on island after island in 1944 and 1945, supported by Navy corpsmen and Army units.

Operation Flintlock began in early February 1944 with a joint Marine-Army assault in the Marshalls at Kwajalein Atoll, followed by a Marine landing 330 miles northwest at Eniwetok Atoll, which consisted of about 30 tiny islands. The three largest were Engebi, Eniwetok, and Parry, and all were intensely defended; aerial photography had proven that the Japanese were slowly building these islands into defensive positions.

Alvin Peachman

The Marshall Islands were beautiful. We came into this atoll, which was one of the most beautiful places I ever saw. The interior [lagoon] was green and the outside reef was like a large ring, never too wide, no more than about a half a mile wide. In some places it was just a few yards, or one hundred yards.

Ralph Leinoff

Kwajalein was a flat island. It was of strategic value because it had an airfield on it, but there was no place for the Japanese to really dig in deep. They had their pillboxes, but they were able to resupply their own ships from Kwajalein, and we had to take it. And we wanted that airfield. So the Navy Air Force did a very good job of bombing the island, so when we got there it was comparatively light resistance. As I say, we had losses, but not on the scale with what was coming up.

The 22ⁿᵈ Regiment of the 6ᵗʰ Marine Division included twenty-one-year-old Joseph Fiore of Glens Falls. He graduated from St. Mary's Academy and enlisted in the Marine Corps in 1942. He described his first encounter with the enemy.

Joe Fiore

I made my first landing on Engebi Island in Eniwetok Atoll. I was scared—yes, I was scared. That was the first island, and the priest heard confessions aboard ship. We were up at four o' clock in the morning, and we went down to the cargo nets into our Higgins boats. But before that, they gave us breakfast, which was a steak with three or four eggs right on top of it, and that was our last meal. Everybody said it was going to be our last meal before we get to get out of here. I was in an amphib [*amphibious landing craft*] with no ramps; we had to go over the side, jump maybe three or four feet from the ground. And all I could think of was, when I jump out of this thing here, I am going to be facing a Jap holding a machine gun on me.

Well, when I hit the ground I looked around and I didn't see anything. We had landed just at the end of the runway that we were there to take because we were 'island hopping,' and every time we took an island, it usually had a runway for planes—our fighter planes. We just start walking on the runway, going up to the other end of the island where headquarters was. Three or four of us were talking as we were walking; we weren't running or anything like that because we didn't see any Japanese. All of a sudden I looked down to the ground and I said, 'Jeeper's sakes, look at those little marks there! They look like Mexican jumping beans!' Well, there were Japanese snipers way back and they were firing, and their bullets were hitting the ground at our feet! We didn't realize it, and then we started running! We made the rest of the island in no time flat. Tony Luciano[21] would've been real proud of me because I broke more records on that day!

We secured the island and spent the night there, which was hectic. That's when the Japs would try to sneak into our positions, but we had machine gunners covering us. The Navy left an awful lot of bomb craters from huge shells, 16-inch shells that exploded on the runway. So we got in those big holes in the ground—it was in the coral reef—and just dug into the side and waited until daylight. When daylight came, then they'd send us back to our ships out in the harbor to get ready for the next operation, which was in the same atoll, Eniwetok Atoll. I would say [the operation] was about four days later, Parry Island, and that's where I got my first Purple Heart.

I used an awful lot of hand grenades in those days. As a matter of fact, I have an article that a war correspondent wrote up on me and called me the 'Pineapple Kid.' I used 70 hand grenades in one day and one night on that island, blowing up foxholes. And underneath the coconut trees, the Japs would build a little nest for themselves, so I was working my way up to an installation that I was going to blow up, and my partner, Seymour Draginsky from New York, Polish Jew, he was backing me up. And a mortar came into our area, and that's when a mortar landed over to my side, and I already had pulled the pin of the grenade. But there's a spoon that goes in the palm of your hand here [gestures], and as long as you keep that grip and that spoon doesn't move, you can walk around the whole island all day long until you're ready to throw it.

---

[21] Legendary Hudson Falls track and field coach, also a World War II Marine veteran and Mr. Fiore's brother-in-law.

Local Marine Hero Called 'Pineapple Kid' by Buddies

(Special to The Post-Star)

SOMEWHERE IN THE PACIFIC —(Delayed)—In the action on Engebi Island, Eniwetok Atoll, Marine Pvt. Joseph P. Fiore, of Glens Falls, N. Y., was known as the "pineapple kid," according to Sgt. Benjamin J. Masselink, a Marine Corps combat correspondent.

In the two days and two nights on Engebi, he used more than 70 hand grenades.

He carried them, along with other explosives, in his pockets, fastened to his dungaree coat, and in a leather Japanese demolition bag which he picked up right after landing on the island.

He did not throw the grenades, but would run up, pull the pin, and merely place the grenade in the opening of an emplacement or underground sniper nest. Then he would step back and wait for the explosion. He put in as many grenades as he thought necessary.

In this manner, he blew up nest after nest throughout the honeycombed island.

One time he ran into a little trouble. A wide awake Jap in a hole threw a grenade back, Pvt. Fiore ducked and rolled in another. The second one came soaring out of the hole. Fiore ducked again and tossed a third. At the same time a Marine standing on a little rise above the hole fired and hit the Jap. The third grenade went off in the hole, finishing the Jap.

Landing with the first wave on Parry Island, Eniwetok Atoll, three days later, Pvt. Fiore was hit in the leg with shrapnel. He was given first aid treatment by Navy corpsmen and taken to the hospital ship.

Pvt. Fiore is the son of Mr. and Mrs. Peter Fiore, 47 Walnut Street

PVT. JOSEPH P. FIORE

Glens Falls Post-Star, May 1, 1944.

So I went down on my stomach in a depression in the ground, and before I knew it, Draginsky had jumped on me because he figured I was wounded. Then I found out later that he was wounded too but he really saved my life. He picked the grenade out of my hand, and he threw it as far as he could and then started dragging me back by my collar. And Sergeant Wolfe came up on the other side, so between them they got me the hell out of that area. A tank was coming up and they put me in the back of the tank, and this corpsman worked on me and got me in a stretcher. And they brought me to the beach, and I ended up on a hospital ship, *USS Solace,* and on my way to Pearl Harbor.

I went to Pearl. I was in there about a month recuperating from the wounds. They gave me that first Purple Heart at Pearl Harbor. As a matter of fact, Admiral Nimitz pinned that on me; someone took a picture of it, and I never saw that picture. I would have loved to have had that!

Walter Hooke had his fill with handling pictures back at the Marshall Islands. He was tasked with a difficult duty—packing up the wallets and personal possessions of those killed in battle to mail home to their families.

Walter Hooke

In the Marshall Islands [*pauses, voice breaking*], I had the job of securing the personal belongings of the guys that were killed, wallets and pictures and dog tags of the guys who were injured or killed. For instance, one of the people I remember making a little box for and wrapping up his wallet and picture of family and parents was the son of Harry Hopkins, who worked as Roosevelt's aide. His son could have been an officer, but he enlisted in the Marine Corps as an ammunition carrier. So I remember making up this little box and sending it to the White House, addressed to Harry Hopkins, with his son's dog tags and wallet....[30]

Stephen Hopkins was just 18. His father was FDR's 'go-to' man in the White House. His commanding officer, Marine Captain Irving Schechter, related the following story after noting his charge's White House address.

Irving Schechter

'Hopkins, I see you have been in officers' training and I'm somewhat puzzled as to why you should show up here. There is no mention of your flunking out of OCS [*Officers Training School*].'

'No, sir,' he answered, 'I did not flunk out; I just got damn sick and tired of getting the needle about my having some kind of an easy job because I was Harry Hopkins's son. My dad has believed in this war since it started and so have his sons. I'm anxious to go overseas and back up what my father stands for because I stand for the same things.'

'Okay, Hopkins,' I told him, 'we'll get you into machine guns in the morning.'

Well, we went into the Roi-Namur part of the Marshalls around the beginning of February. Our battalion went ashore on Namur... whenever you have to kill a few thousand Japanese, you always lose men yourself. One of the Marines we lost here was young Hopkins. He had kept his machine gun going right into the middle of a banzai charge until he took a bullet in his head.[31]

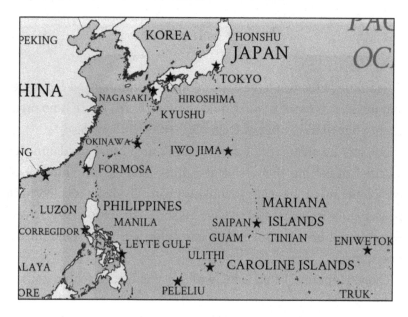

The Marianas and environs.

The Marianas—Saipan, Guam, and Tinian

Fiore lost his original outfit and took up duties in the 2ⁿᵈ Marine Division as a flamethrower for the invasion of Saipan in the Marianas. In mid-June 1944, just over a week after the Normandy landings in France, 20,000 Marines of the 2ⁿᵈ and 4ᵗʰ Divisions landed and suffered heavy casualties. Reserves of Marine battalions and the Army's 27ᵗʰ Division followed a few days later.

Ralph Leinoff

In the Marianas, we had the islands of Saipan and Tinian. Now that's getting close—they were about 1,500 miles south of Japan. You had to go up and down these valleys and there was a lot of vegetation in there. Now the island is only about 18 miles long. It's shaped something like an upside-down monkey wrench. You know what a monkey wrench looks like? You turn it upside-down you got an idea of what Saipan was like. It had a sugar mill and they had agriculture. It was a very beautiful island, actually... These are not coral islands, now. The Marianas were actually sandy beach islands, and we were able to get in with faster vehicles, but of course the amount of fire that we took was enormous, compared to what happened at Kwajalein.

The Japanese managed to stake out a number of snipers and they took their toll. And it was very hard to find out where we were being shot at from, so we took a lot more losses on Saipan. We lost a lot of men there getting on that island, and that took more than five days. It took us about three weeks or so to get up to the north end of the island, and in that three weeks we suffered casualties, but less and less each day. The worst casualties were suffered by the Army, which went up a low section of the island. The Japanese had reformed and it was a nasty battle between so-called banzai fighters and the Army. They were able to break through the Army lines and get all the way back to the Marine Corps artillery. It was Marine artillery that would stop them.

The Marines on Saipan were joined by the Army's 27th Infantry Division, a New York National Guard unit federalized in October 1940. Many of its members hailed from the mill towns north of Albany, and it was the 27th which would bear the brunt of the biggest banzai attack of the war.[32] Before the final attack, the Marine commander expressed his unhappiness in front of war correspondents with the progress of the Army soldiers, and had the Army general relieved of his command. In fact, in the attack to follow, three members of the 105th Regiment would be awarded the Medal of Honor, posthumously.[33]

Nicholas Grinaldo of Troy was a twenty-three–year-old sergeant who would receive two Purple Hearts and the Bronze Star for his actions on Saipan. In an interview with the NYS Military Museum's Veterans Oral History Project, he explained the situation.

Nick Grinaldo

The 27th Division got stuck in the mountains fighting. We had to fight cave to cave, hand to hand sometimes. And we had a General Smith, Ralph Smith, one hell of a good man. And he was relieved by this Marine general, 'Howlin' Mad' [*Holland M.*] Smith. From what I understood back then, the reason he was relieved of his command was that the Marines said we could not keep up with them. Well, Jesus Christ, they had tank support down in the lowlands, which we didn't have! They confiscated half of the 27th's artillery... and we were supposed to keep up with them! The best we had was 60 and 81mm mortars, and half the time you could not use them because of the terrain. There were mountains, gulches, hillsides, caves dug into them. That's the way it was, it was really rough going up through the goddamn mountains! As much as you tried, you could not keep up with them. You go past a cave so small you never noticed the opening. The next thing you know, you're getting shot at from behind.

John Sidur was a twenty-six–year-old sergeant from Cohoes, New York, and would also receive the Bronze Star for his bravery at Saipan.

John Sidur

We had this cave, and we had two Japanese [*Japanese-American*] guys from the Hawaiian Islands; they didn't carry any guns or anything, but they were smart. They walked right into the cave and talked to the Japanese soldiers. They weren't going to give up. Our two came out and told us, and then went back in and told them they had five minutes before we are going to shell them. Then they went back in and told them they had three minutes—all of a sudden we heard the screaming of women and children! We told them to let the civilians out. The Japanese wouldn't let them out—that was their protection. So it came down to... they blew the cave up! How many people were killed, we don't know, but that cave was closed. They exploded it with dynamite!

On July 7, after three weeks of fighting, the worst suicide charge of the Pacific War was about to get underway. Rather than resort to surrender, between three and five thousand screaming Japanese soldiers and sailors broke through a gap in the Army lines.

Nick Grinaldo

I remember it rained like hell that night, and the water was running down the slope into our foxholes. I had to use my helmet to keep bailing out, you know. The night before the banzai, I woke up that morning and, oh, Jesus Christ, they [the Japanese] got above us, and they were giving us plunging fire, shooting right down into the foxholes, because they were high enough to look down. Lt. Gower, he was my platoon leader, he was regular Army...he was a good man. He called us together, the squad leaders. He said, 'I think we're getting hit with a banzai. We're going to have to pull back.' Holy Jesus, there was howling and screaming! They had naked women, with spears, stark naked! They took bayonets and strapped them on the end of a pole. And they came screaming at us, figuring, 'Hey, the good-hearted Americans ain't gonna shoot a woman, you know?' Horseshit. There were so many of them, like cockroaches coming out of the woodwork. We had to pull back.

John Sidur

I saw everything, women and men mixed up, everything, and we just kept shooting. Whoever got too close, that's who got the bullet... we got to the point that there were too many casualties. So we tried to hold back as much as we could. We were getting mixed up with the Japanese, and all of a sudden we got hit with artillery. American artillery. They said it was for the Japanese, but we were on the frontline and we got hit with that. We lost quite a few men— I got hit then, I got shrapnel from artillery on my hand, not too bad.

Nick Grinaldo

I was with the lieutenant and a few of the men that were with me. And all of a sudden I turn around and I see the lieutenant go down. He took one right across here [*gestures to his jaw*], blew the whole bottom of his jaw right off... I went to grab him, to take him with us. And he said, [*shaking his head*] 'Get back to the Japanese trenches!' There were trenches at the point, that's where we headed... it was general rout, a general rout. We had them running right alongside of us. I had one running right alongside of me. Christ, he wasn't five feet from me! I don't know whether he was 'sakeed up' or what the hell was wrong with him, but I put him down quickly, I tell you![22] They were right with us!

That's when I got shot through the shoulder. When we fell back to the trenches, my rifle fell out of my hand, and I went to pick it up; I could not close my hand. I looked and I saw a trickle of blood

---

[22] sake-Japanese 'rice wine' alcoholic beverage

on my right shoulder. We had a guy by the name of Tony Simonds, he was in C Company before he went to a medical detachment. And [now] he was running with us, and he turned around and he said, 'Let me fix your arm, sergeant.' I said, 'Not here, Jesus Christ, not here!' He said, 'Here, you're hurt bad!' He took care of me. While he's standing in front of me, he took one [*a bullet*] right in the back which was intended for me—he took it. Nice guy, a real nice guy.

We got to the Jap trenches all right, and all of a sudden we started to get hit with artillery fire. Real bad, and it was our own! They had to be [105mm] howitzers, and they poured them into us, trying to break up the Jap banzai.

27th Division on Saipan assessing results following July 7, 1944 banzai charge. New York State Military Museum.

That's what they tried, to break up the attack. Unfortunately, we had made it back there and they didn't know we were there, and they killed [us]—half of the casualties we suffered were right there.

More than 900 men of the 27th Division's 105th Regiment would be killed or wounded in this attack. With their backs to the water, the Army survivors could see half of the estimated 4,300 Japanese dead in front of them.[34]

When the Saipan operation was declared secure on July 9, over 16,500 Americans were casualties, with over 3,400 killed or missing. Approximately 29,000 Japanese defenders had been killed, with almost no prisoners being taken. Some of the enemy survivors would live on in the hills for months and even years afterwards.[35] To compound the horror, over twenty thousand civilians were killed, hundreds of whom committed suicide by wading into the sea or jumping off cliffs, fearful of U.S. soldiers and captivity.

Ralph Leinoff

The native population, the Chamorros, had been under Japanese control for many years, and they were fed a lot of propaganda about how they should not surrender to the Americans, the American troops are barbarians and everything. And rather than surrender—they believed this stuff—and we tried to get women and children down, but the people were so indoctrinated that rather than surrender, they jumped from the cliffs with...with the babes. There are movies—you might've seen them, I don't know—showing people who were trying to get them down and they wouldn't trust us.

Joe Fiore

The Japanese told these people there that if the Americans grab you, they are going to torture you and kill you, especially Marines, because in order to become a Marine you had to kill either your mother or your father, which was garbage. But those people 'ate it,' and they jumped, they jumped off that cliff! Terrible!

Joe Fiore would be one of the American casualties in the battle for Saipan.

I was wounded here [*points to chin*] and took one here [*points to lower lip/jaw*], and, of course, from my ankle to my buttocks, it was full of shrapnel. That hurt! And I didn't realize how much shrapnel I had in me until they got me off the stretcher, these two hospital corpsmen, and they sat me in these metal chairs. Well, I went right through the ceiling! It was like sitting on a pin cushion... I was in isolation because of my wounds. The most serious one went in here and came out here [*points to upper thigh*]. It was a piece of shrapnel. So I was in tough shape. For 18 days, I was out of it. I was receiving morphine every 12 hours—at noon and at midnight—and it would wear off at 10 o'clock, right on the dot. And I'd beg the nurse to give me another shot, and she said, 'No way!'

So anyway, I finally got out of there and back to my outfit, and I was back in combat again. And when I left the hospital, I still had a bandage around this leg [*points to left thigh*].

My mother took it pretty bad when she got the telegram that I was wounded. So my sister and my brother said, 'Well, Ma, at least he's alive!' And I felt sorry for her when she got the notice of the second Purple Heart... [*He trails off, looks down, and softly begins to cry*].

Fiore shortly returned stateside on leave and finished out the war in the Philadelphia Navy Yard. Even before the battles had ended at Saipan, Guam, and Tinian, Navy Seabees got to work and the first B–29 bombers arrived.

The Hell of Peleliu

Working his way out of Australia, General MacArthur prepared for his assault on the Philippine Islands. Military planners decided early on that the fortified island of Peleliu stood in the way and would have to be taken. On September 15, 1944, the 1ˢᵗ Marine Division and Army troops began the attack on Peleliu after three days of heavy bombardment by Navy gunships. Peleliu hosted a major Japanese airfield that, in the planning stages, was deemed a major threat to any U. S. advance on the Philippines. The island was heavily defended by over 13,500 Imperial troops dug into a network of pillboxes and 500 coral caverns and caves.

Four young men from the local counties surrounding the "Falls" back home were assigned to the 1ˢᵗ Marine Division and had developed a strong bond even before going overseas. They now found themselves together in the thick of it on Peleliu, and later, would be in the battle for Okinawa. Daniel Lawler was assigned as an ammunition carrier in a squad for a BAR [Browning automatic rifle, a .30–caliber heavy machine gun] to K Company, 3ʳᵈ Battalion, 5ᵗʰ Regiment.[23] John W. 'Jack' Murray was a squad leader and heavy machine gunner. Harold Chapman joined Jim Butterfield in the 6ᵗʰ Company, 2ⁿᵈ Battalion, 1ˢᵗ Regiment.
Dan Lawler was nineteen years old.

Dan Lawler

We hit the island, which was only four miles long by two miles wide. I was in the first assault wave. It was hell, and everyone was scared—it was an awful feeling. As we disembarked, I looked up and down the beaches, and all you could hear was screaming, and men were falling and dying. There was artillery, mortar, and machine

---

[23] One of the main outfits portrayed in the 2010 HBO series, *The Pacific*.

gun fire constantly. We fought all day, and by evening, we reached the airstrip about half a mile from the beach. We set up for the night along the sides of the airstrip. The temperature was from 102° at night to 120° in the daytime.

We went in with two canteens of water—that's a gallon of water. This island was two degrees off the equator! By noontime, we were out of water. They sent more in to us in 40-gallon drums. They brought them up to the lines, and we drew the water out. They used these for gasoline before, and didn't clean them out—so we almost got sick just drinking water.

John Murray

Luckily, we made it to the far side of the field. My squad was still intact. The first thing I saw was a Japanese machine gunner chained to his machine gun... They were not going to give up.

Dan Lawler

The second day in, I started across the airfield, and machine gun fire and shells were going by us. We were running, and what you do is run a short distance and then you drop, run a short distance and then you drop. You never want to stay running, because you do not want the Japs' machine guns to get after you. About halfway across, I heard an artillery piece go off. It must have landed behind me, and I went down—face down. When I woke up I was still facing down. I pulled my right hand down, and I looked at it [*looks at hand*]. It was all bloody, and I couldn't feel anything in it. So the corpsman came along, and he said, 'You have four fingers broken.' And my arm was broken [*points to arm*]. So he patched that much up and said, 'You also got hit in the back—you got a wound on your back.' So he patched that up, tagged me, and then I came out.

Dan Lawler, 2011. Portrait by Robert H. Miller.

Lawler was evacuated to a hospital ship, then to a hospital on Guadal-canal. He was awarded the Purple Heart and rejoined his outfit later on Pavuvu, the 'rest and recuperation' area back in the Solomons.

John Murray

Some of our men were getting hit and we were much smaller now. There was no clean water on the island, and our water was brought in old oil drums that hadn't been properly cleaned. Between the bad water and the extreme heat, many of us started to get sick with dysentery and fungus. I believe time on the island under these conditions was starting to take its toll. The 1st and 7th Marines were out of action because of casualties. We, the 5th Marines, had to take Bloody Nose Ridge.

After securing the airstrip, the Marines headed into the coral hills to reduce the Japanese defenders. The fight for Bloody Nose Ridge and the Umurbrogol Mountain was particularly brutal, and considered one of the most difficult fights of the entire war, with the 1ˢᵗ Division losing up to one-third of its strength. Many of the hundreds of limestone caves and former mine shafts were interconnected and had multiple entrances, housing artillery pieces protected by sliding steel doors, machine guns, and thousands of troops.[36]

Jim Butterfield

The first 200 hours at Peleliu, we lost over 1,600 people. That made our regiment the first regiment that could no longer function as a regiment! They split the rest of us up—which was about 500—into other outfits.

John Murray

My memory of what happened was of total destruction and death. Every day was the same. That damned island was all coral rock. Our movement was slow, sometimes only a few yards each day... It's hazy now but it was very vivid for so long, sleepless nights filled with emptiness, sadness, fear, and total anger, constant yelling, flares in the sky all the time, spurts from our machine guns. I know I prayed a lot, held my rosary around my neck. We prayed and remembered our relentless training and hoped the two would pull us through. And as the days went by, I realized that there was a strong possibility I wouldn't get off Peleliu alive.

We started up the ridge October 6. As we pressed toward the top, flamethrowers were necessary to get those animals out of the caves. The closer we got to the top, the more resistance we faced.

Our second lieutenant tried to go over the top, but got hit in the shoulder and had to be moved out. Machine gunners were given orders to spray the ridges, especially the caves where the bastards hid.

Our squad had been hit hard. There were 15 of us on September 15, and now there were five of us left and most of us were sick. I turned around and asked for more ammunition, and I only had five more rounds left. I hadn't realized my right knee was exposed; something made my left ear ring. I looked down and saw that my right knee had been shot off by a sniper hidden in a cave. I lay flat on the ground so he couldn't get another good shot at me. They located the cave, and a flamethrower came up and filled the cave with flames. That Jap came running out, flames all over him—completely engulfed. I fired a burst at him. It was all over then.[37]

Casualties were very heavy. The 1ˢᵗ Marine Division lost 1,252 killed and over 5,700 wounded or missing. The 81ˢᵗ Infantry Division, sent in to relieve the Marines, lost over 540 dead and 2,700 wounded or missing in action. The battle remains controversial since it was never used as a staging area for the invasion of the Philippines or any other subsequent operations, though it did draw some Japanese troops away from the Philippines. Nearly 10,700 Japanese were killed on the tiny island.

Jim Butterfield

You've got to stop and remember when you're studying about these islands that the Japanese had ten years of war before we got into it, before they bombed Pearl Harbor. They were at China, Korea, and other places over there. These people were good. On these islands, they were digging [fortifications] for years! They didn't meet you out on the beaches; we had to go get them. They knew what we were going to do, and they were good.

The purpose at Peleliu was to take that airport and securely keep it. It was also to draw troops from the Philippines. MacArthur was getting ready to go in there. I guess we pulled a couple of divisions out. Peleliu, in the last five years, has come forward to become one of the biggest battles of the Pacific. In fact, after we secured Peleliu, it came out in *Time Magazine* with MacArthur that it wasn't really necessary that we took Peleliu. Now this doesn't make you feel too good, when all your friends are gone, but it brought back some memories. I was up there for 74 days, and fortunately, I did not get wounded. I lost part of my hearing up there, but otherwise I came out pretty good. It was the [bitterest] battle of the Marine Corps in World War II. There's no doubt about it.[38]

CHAPTER NINE

Captivity-Year 3

The Hellships

As the Marines prepared for combat on Peleliu, Robert Blakeslee was herded with 750 other American prisoners aboard a decrepit prison ship for transport to Japan for slave labor. Nearly 19,000 men were transported in the stifling holds of these unmarked 'hellships,' destined to be used by Japanese industrialists for slave labor. At least sixty percent of these prisoners never made it to Japan alive due to submarine and air attacks, unsanitary and inhumane conditions, and the brutal treatment of their captors[39].

After 28 months in captivity and 19 days of brutal conditions in the bottom of the hold of the transport, Blakeslee's ship would be torpedoed by the *USS Paddle*, an American submarine. He would be one of only 83 survivors, as he later relayed in a 1945 debriefing.

Robert Blakeslee

During the summer [of 1944], we began to hear rumors that we might be shipped to Japan—we heard that the men in No. 2 Camp at Davao had been shipped out early in June. The Japs were getting uneasy and we were pretty sure the Yanks were getting near. We knew they had taken over the Solomons and that they were in New Guinea. This airfield they made us work on was a re-fueling point for planes being ferried southward, and it bristled with anti-aircraft guns. When we learned of bullet-riddled Jap planes arriving at a nearby navy air field, we knew for sure the Yanks were not too far away.

Finally, on August 5, they told us to get ready to move. They said we were to be taken to Japan and put aboard an exchange ship to be exchanged for Japanese nationals that were U.S. prisoners. I guess we only half-believed that story, but in any case, Lasang [*Japanese airfield*] seemed like a good place to be away from. You see, we figured if the Yanks moved in, either one of two things probably would happen: the Japs would shoot all of us, or a lot of us would get killed trying to make a break for freedom.

They gave us back the shoes we had gotten from the Red Cross way back in February, and the last of four packages of food, candy, cigarettes that had arrived at the same time. We had worn those shoes only a month when there was an escape from the camp and they were taken away. From then on, we were barefoot. Incidentally, those shoes upset the Jap soldiers. They had rubber soles and heels. Their officers had told them America didn't have any rubber.

As it turned out, we had our shoes back only for one day. The Japanese major who had been in command moved out, leaving a first lieutenant in command. Also, he cut us down to two meals a day, one of rice and salt and the other a pasty mixture of camotes, something like a sweet potato, and squash. We were on that diet for two weeks.

During that time we saw the first Allied planes we had seen since before the fall of Bataan. There were air raid alerts nearly every night, and one night a single multi-motored plane came over and we heard bomb explosions nearby. It was one of the sweetest sounds I've ever heard!

On August 20 they told us for the second time to get ready to move. They roused us at three the next morning, and after a scanty meal of rice with a little meat and salt in it, they lined us up in lines of fours with about 175 men in a group. Then they strung a heavy rope around the outside of the group, tying it to all the men on the outside of the column. Anyone who stepped outside the rope would be shot, they said.

Ringed by guards armed with bayoneted rifles and with a truck containing a machine gun detail ahead and behind each group, we marched three miles to the dock. There we were joined by another hundred American prisoners who had been in the custody of the Jap navy. They gave us back our shoes, but told us not to put them on.

The Holds of Hell

We were loaded in barges and taken out to a freighter of about 5,000 tons that was anchored in Davao Gulf. After climbing up rope ladders we were herded into two holds, about 450 men in one and 300 in the other. I was in the larger group.

As soon as we were packed in, they pulled up the ladder and covered up the hatch, all but a strip about two feet wide along each side. Each hatch was guarded by a detail of soldiers armed with a machine gun, rifles, and grenades. It was pretty obvious that if anything happened to the ship, they had no intention of letting any of us get out.

There we were, just like rats in a trap, in an area about 50 by 60 feet. The only light and air came from those two strips alongside the hatches. It was about 110 degrees down there, and to make things worse, the vessel's last cargo had been salt, which got in the cracks and sores on our feet. There was one small ventilator in the hold, but it didn't work.

We had been given a mess kit of rice before leaving the camp, and late in the afternoon they sent down some water. But at that point we weren't very well organized; some got a lot and others got none.

Some of the men had brought native brooms with them, and finally we got organized, got the hold swept out and arranged so everyone could lie down. The men lay like sardines, one man's feet alongside another's head.

There were no water facilities for washing, or for latrines. They sent down some five-gallon gasoline cans to use for latrines. The task of emptying those became a choice assignment because it gave those who did it a chance to get up in the fresh air for a few minutes.

As the afternoon wore on, it got hotter and hotter. In the evening, one man cracked and began screaming for water. The Japs had told us that if there were any disturbances they would fire on us. We were pretty apprehensive about that, but one of the men who spoke a little Japanese succeeded in convincing the guards that the man was delirious and not responsible for his actions. He was still delirious the next day and finally the medical officer in our group gave him drugs from his pitifully small stock to keep him quiet.

The next morning they passed down our first meal, a small portion of steamed rice and a watery soup made of camotes and a little water. They promised us a canteen of water per man as a daily ration, but we never got that much. Generally the ration was less than a pint. That morning the Japs began practicing air raid alerts. Each time they would cover over the hatch completely, cutting off what little air and light there was.

In the afternoon there was a real air raid. We heard the plane, then the chattering of machine guns, the boom of anti-aircraft, and finally the concussion of bombs. The concussions were near enough so that they nearly caused a panic. Then the chaplain took over. He was a chaplain who had been decorated for valor at Clark Field. Setting an example by his calmness, he urged the men to be quiet, that it was better that way, since there was nothing they could do. Then he said a prayer.

After that, he conducted a vesper service every evening, and sometimes, one of the officers, who was a first-rate story teller, would narrate the story of some book he had read.

The men were organized in groups of 25 for the distribution of food and water. That ensured everyone getting a share. Because there was so little air, four periods a day were set aside for smoking. Then we would all wave towels to get the smoke out of the hold. There were two meals a day, and actually most of our days were taken up waiting in line to be served, or waiting our turn at the gasoline cans that served as latrines.

The first night the vessel had anchored in Davao Gulf, but about 2:00 a.m. the second night, it began to move again. The Japs immediately covered over the hatches. By morning, 70 of the men were unconscious. We moved them to the area directly under the hatch where the best air was, and they were there in the morning when the Japs came down to count us—they counted us twice a day, God only knows why! I guess they realized then how bad the air was, for after that they opened up the hatch a little more. Some of the men had shelter tent halves, and they built makeshift wind scoops out of them. The Jap guards set them up above the hatch but they didn't work too well.

The second morning, they had let us up on deck in groups of 50 for about ten minutes of calisthenics, but after that air raid, they wouldn't let us up anymore. The third morning, as we were steaming out of Davao Gulf, we heard explosions like depth charges, but we never did find out whether there had been a sub attack, or if it was just an anti-submarine drill staged by the three naval vessels that were escorting our ship. To tell the truth, we weren't too worried about submarines. We figured that American submarines had been notified when we sailed—but the Japs crossed us up.

By the fourth day, we had become so dehydrated and were suffering so from thirst that we finally prevailed upon the Japs to substitute lugao, a gruel-like rice preparation, instead of the drier boiled rice. I'll never forget how good it tasted. But despite that slight change, men were passing out constantly from heat and thirst. The medical officer and the chaplain spent most of their time attending to them. About all that could be done was to move them to the area beneath the hatch, fan them, and put salt water compresses on them. They were about the only medical cases those first days. Fortunately, there was no dysentery. That would have been terrible!

Here's how the Japs crossed us up. We pulled into a harbor, lay there for nine days, then they transferred us to another freighter [the *Shinyo Maru*]. During those nine days we were on deck three times, once for 10 minutes of calisthenics and twice to stand briefly under a salt water hose.

The _Shinyo Maru_ before 1936. USN.

We thought that first freighter was awful, but once they transferred us, things got even worse. The first carried a cargo of hemp that filled the lower part of the hold. The second had nothing but some rock ballast, and we were right down on the keel, about 30 feet below the deck. The hold I was in was about the same size as the previous one, but instead of 450 of us, they jammed in 500. It was so crowded, all of us couldn't lie down at once. We had to sleep in shifts. We couldn't even organize lines to the latrines. Instead, those cans had to be passed through our area from man to man.

The vessel apparently had carried a cargo of cement not too long before, and our movements raised a cloud of cement dust. It filled our nostrils, caked on our perspiring bodies, and went in our hair and beards. As soon as we got down there, they placed boards over the hatch, leaving a little space between them for air, and then lashed them down. We were there 24 hours before sailing.

Right after we started, the Japs began having practice alerts. Each time they would throw a tarpaulin over the hatch, shutting out the light and most of the air. So actually, the heat, filth, and air were worse than on the other ship. And in addition to the exhaustion cases, some of the men had malaria attacks and others developed skin diseases.

Torpedoed

About 5:30 on the afternoon of September 7, we heard some small arms fire, then the bugler blowing an alert. We could tell this was the real thing from the way he blew. Can you imagine how a man might blow a bugle with his teeth chattering? Well, that's just the way it sounded. I remember thinking that just before everything went blank. I heard no explosion, no outcries.

The next thing I remember, it couldn't have been more than a few seconds later, and I was fighting salt water. For what seemed like minutes, I seemed to be suspended like in mid-air, and then I shot upward! I had barely time to fill my lungs before I was sucked down again. On the way down I grabbed a piece of rope. When I came to the surface again I was near the top of the hold, which was nearly completely submerged. I just swam out and away from the side of the ship, grabbing at various floating objects. It was then that I discovered my right arm was useless. I finally caught the edge of a piece of a life raft and glimpsed eight or ten other prisoners clutching it also. Bullets were hitting the water all around us. They were fired by Japs standing in a lifeboat on the freighter!

The freighter, hit by one torpedo in the bow, apparently right in the hold that I was in, and by a second torpedo just ahead of the aft hold, sank in about ten minutes.

Just as they cast off their lifeboat, it capsized and the Japs joined us in the water. Among them was the sadistic lieutenant who had been in charge of us at the airfield after the major left. Looking at him, I remembered the pleasure he seemed to get out of meting out punishment for minor infractions of rules. Once, I recalled, he tortured a group of about 50 men by making them kneel for about 45 minutes with their shins on the sharp flange of a railway rail. Now he didn't look so brave. If I ever saw a man look afraid, he was the one.

Through an interpreter, he told us that if we would not harm the Japanese, he personally would guarantee our safety. As if we didn't know what his guarantee was worth, we saw one of the Jap escort vessels moving toward us, picking up survivors—Jap survivors! They were shooting whatever Americans they saw!

It was obvious there was no safety in numbers on that raft, and some of the men began to swim away. Finally there were three of us left. One of the men and I were constantly bobbing back and forth under the raft trying to keep it between ourselves and the Jap marksmen aboard the naval vessel. The other man was either injured or did not realize the danger, for he merely clung to the raft without making any effort at concealment. Suddenly I looked up and noted there were only two of us. Where the third man had been there was a neat bullet hole in the raft!

When darkness hid us from the Jap vessel, my companion and I climbed up on the raft, both of us pretty exhausted. I apparently went to sleep immediately. The moon was up when I awoke. We decided we had best try to paddle our piece of raft toward shore. I quickly found there wasn't much I could do because of my useless arm. And every time my companion tried, he would break into a spasm of coughing and would spit blood. Besides, the current was against us.

Through the night we floated aimlessly amid the wreckage. At daylight, we observed we were floating in the approximate area where the prison ship had gone down. Once again we tried to paddle toward shore, but made scant headway. By noon the sun was hot and blistering and we were parched with thirst. We had no food or water.

Suddenly we saw two Filipinos in a banca boat [outrigger canoe] a short distance away, and we hollered to them. They acknowledged our shouts by waving, but would not come near us. In desperation, we began furiously to paddle toward them. The Filipinos packed up their paddles and moved away. Jap planes were passing over from time to time and apparently they were afraid they would be observed aiding us.

By mid-afternoon we decided we had best abandon the raft in favor of life preservers, several of which were floating around. My companion, by this time, was getting very weak. I finally spotted a preserver and we swam toward it only to find that it supported a dead Jap. My companion removed the Jap, donned the preserver, and started off alone. To my knowledge, that is the last anyone saw him.

After experimenting with some floating boards, I finally elected to stay with the raft another night. I was on the verge of delirium by this time, and while I slept some, the night was a horrible experience. Toward dawn, however, I slept soundly and awoke refreshed and much stronger. A stiff wind had come up during the night and blown my raft down the coast about 20 miles, I learned later. I was still two or three miles from shore and headed toward the open sea. It was obvious my only chance lay in heading toward shore at once. I struggled all morning, pushing and pulling the raft, but made scant progress. I was about to give up in despair when I heard an American voice behind me.

I looked around. There was a smiling Yank, astride a big bamboo raft, with a smaller one tied behind it. He was Pvt. D.J. Olinger of Denver, Colorado. He had found the raft soon after being blown overboard.

We decided to wait until night and then try to paddle the smaller raft toward shore. Late in the afternoon, we saw some bancas close to shore, and two finally appeared behind us. After we convinced them we were Americans, they went for aid. While they were gone, some others appeared that had room in their craft and they took us ashore just as darkness fell. That was the evening of September 9.

We were taken inland and fed a mixture of raw eggs and put to bed. The next day we had a virtual banquet: rice, boiled chicken, goats' milk, and more eggs. They told us some other survivors had come ashore, and in the afternoon some guerrillas came and took us to them. There were six other survivors there, two with compound leg fractures. A Filipino doctor attended a dozen or so lacerations, but since he had no anesthetic, he could do nothing for my injured arm.

Within a few days, more survivors arrived, until finally there were 83 of us, including 25 officers. Twenty-eight of us, all of whom had been in that forward hold, had broken eardrums. As nearly as we could gather, the torpedo had struck just about midway along the side of the hold.

It was the third night, October 30, before contact was made with the sub, and shortly thereafter we saw its dark outline in the water. Some of its crew came ashore with rubber boats to take the litter cases aboard. The others were taken out in bancas. We arrived in New Guinea, where we were feted at a naval base with the most delicious steak I've ever tasted, French-fried potatoes, and cold beer from Terre Haute, Indiana.

A short time later, I was flown to Australia for hospitalization. While there, I was promoted to major. I had been promoted to captain a month before the fall of Bataan. Several of us arrived back in the U.S. together November 6 and went to Washington, where we were awarded Purple Hearts. I was assigned to Walter Reed Hospital, and it was there that I saw my wife for the first time in more than three years. A couple of weeks later, my son Stephen joined us in Albany. He was 15 months old when I left. Now he is four and a half!

I lost everything when the prison ship went down, including my most prized possession. It was a New Testament, bearing a Jap censor's stamp: 'Approved reading.'[40]

*

Joe Minder dared to hope at the arrival of American planes overhead, but would soon find himself in his own version of hell.

Joe Minder

March 29 to August 14, 1944

Morale is as low as a snake's back around here. Many men have taken sick and have been sent to Bilibid hospital for treatment, but many have died soon after arriving there because of their terrible condition when they leave here. Several other men, however, have deliberately broken their arms and legs to get away from the hard work and brutal treatment on the airfield.

August 19 to September 20, 1944

Working building plane revetments [*reinforced parking areas*]. Neck stiff as heck from blows from the fists of "Higison," a very small Jap guard. First he slapped me in the face until it was numb, then belted me a couple good 'haymakers' to the jaw.

September 21, 1944

Planes! Planes! American planes! All heck broke loose directly overhead when the Americans slipped in through the clouds, contacted Jap planes, and started several dogfights all around us! We ran from the field to a mango grove and saw what we had been waiting for. The dogfights lasted for about one hour. During that time we saw the Yanks shoot down one large transport plane, and they sent several Jap fighter planes away smoking! With all the Jap planes driven off, our Grumman Navy planes started diving on the bay and Nichols Field and all the other military objectives, strafing and bombing with no opposition air at all! Several stray 20-millimeter shells landed 25 yards from us in the mango grove, but we were so darned excited watching our planes we didn't even go for a hole. We were darn lucky that the Americans did not frog bomb and strafe under the trees where we were! When they strafed the fields, hundreds of Japs and Filipinos working on the field ran under the grove. They must have been visible from the air.

September 22, 1944

American planes came back at 8:00 a.m. and continued their heavy bombings of Nichols Field and Manila Bay. With only about five miles from the bombing point, we can feel the ground shake under us when these huge explosives go off, caused by exploding ammunition dumps and boats in the bay! Huge billows of smoke and fire rising high into the air can be clearly seen from here. Everyone is excited wondering how long it will be before the Yanks land on Luzon and free us. Many of us, however, are wondering if any of our American POW friends were killed at Nichols Field.

8:00 p.m.

The sky just lit up for a second when a terrific explosion went off in the Manila area, making the doors rattle in our barracks!

September 23 to September 30, 1944

Having it pretty easy now working in stone quarry and laying stone on airfield. Also getting pretty good food again.

39 Days in the Hole

October 1, 1944: 2:00 p.m.

Oh, what misery! Seven hundred forty-one of us are packed into the forward hold of a small, crummy coal cargo ship sitting here in Manila Bay waiting to be shipped to Japan! We are packed into a small space of 35 feet by 50 feet almost on top of one another!

6:00 p.m.

Several old letters were just brought aboard from Manila. Most of them have been here for months! I received several Christmas cards from people in North Creek in December 1943, also some letters from home; one had a nice picture of my ma and dad.

I know this is going to be hell, standing down here in this cramped position for twelve days, but after seeing those pictures and reading those letters and cards, I don't feel quite so bad now.

October 3, 1944

Finally moving out of the bay in a small merchant convoy of Jap ships. The bay is full of wrecked ships which the Americans sank in the September 21 and 22 air raids. With no markings on this tub whatsoever, we are expected to be sent to the bottom any day now by a Yank bomb or a torpedo! No one has a life belt, and there is only one small escape ladder running down to this stuffy, crowded hold, three decks below the top of the ship, so our chances of surviving are darn small if the Yanks sink this scow! With only a couple small machine guns on it, the Yanks can also strafe the heck out of us if they so desire.

October 9, 1944: 2:00 p.m.

Ten men have already died from overcrowded conditions and lack of water and have been thrown overboard. We thought we might be some more shark bait a few minutes ago when the Yank sub fired a torpedo at us, barely missing the bow of the ship, and sank an oil tanker along the side of us. When the Japs started dropping depth charges, it sounded like the sides would collapse in on us!

October 10, 1944

Carl Deamer died last night in my arms. He passed out several times last night with a high fever. I managed to bring him to several times by fanning the heck out of him, but about 5:00 a.m., Carl's worries ended. I first met him at Camp I in November 1942.

October 11, 1944

Sailed into Hong Kong harbor.

October 12 to October 21, 1944

Started sailing out of the bay for Formosa [Taiwan]. Sure glad to leave here! Americans have visited this place several times with their bombs and have bombed many of the buildings on the waterfront and have left the bay full of bomb-blasted ships. We were bombed once, but luckily the Yanks missed us again. We unloaded copra and have sugar aboard now.

October 25, 1944

Arrived at Port Takao in Formosa.

November 8, 1944

After being chased in and out of the bay by the American bombers, we are finally going ashore this morning!

10:00 p.m.

Just got on shore, most of us are so weak we can barely walk! During those 39 days of hell, cramped up in that crummy hole, we lost 38 of our men. The rest of us who managed to survive have lost many pounds. God! What [awful] looking men! With a 39-day beard, dirty, pale, and skinny, we all look like walking skeletons coming out of a dungeon!

Like Joe and thousands of others, John Parsons had arrived in Formosa from the Philippines on a hellship two years earlier. During this time the men captured with him at Bataan labored at working in rice fields, growing sweet potatoes, and making rope. He remembered that 'on rainy days, the camp would be called out and made to sit in a group on the wet ground facing mounted machine guns. [We] were told that in the event of an Allied invasion of Formosa, this would be [our] fate. This took place about once a week, and having no source of news, [we] never knew if it was the real thing or another rehearsal.'

Just before Joe Minder arrived at Takao, John was leaving that port on another hellship bound for Japan, a route that Joe would be following soon enough. The Oyroku Maru had considerable difficulty getting out of the

Formosa harbor. The prisoners were packed into their compartments with timbers wedged against the door and the hatches sealed as the harbor endured three days of consecutive bombing by American planes. One bomb struck so close that it killed 17 Japanese soldiers on the deck. The first attempt to leave the harbor ended when a submarine was detected the first night out and the hellship turned back; the men remained confined aboard and forced to wait in the harbor for another five days. On the second attempt, a torpedo narrowly missed the ship and exploded on the shoreline. The vessel finally made it out of the harbor and on its way to Japan only with the help of a destroyer escort.[41] *Two months later, the Oyroku Maru was bombed off the Philippines in Subic Bay with 1,600 American prisoners on board. Survivors were forced into the water and many were deliberately machine gunned before they could reach shore.*

John Parsons would spend the remainder of his captivity at the notorious Mukden POW camp in the far reaches of Manchuria. He would be liberated by Soviet troops on August 20, 1945.

CHAPTER TEN

The Sands of Iwo Jima

As the tens of thousands of prisoners were being transported to
the Japanese home islands for slave labor and the Philippines was
slowly being liberated, military planners focused on the next two
stepping stones—Iwo Jima and Okinawa.

Iwo Jima, or 'Sulfur Island,' was eight square miles of sand, ash,
and rock lying 660 miles southeast of Tokyo. It could serve as a re-
fueling stop for the B–29s and B–24s that were now flying almost
daily out of the fields in the Marianas to bomb the Japanese mainland. In late November 1944, aerial bombardment of Iwo Jima with
high explosives began and continued for a record 74 straight days.
The 21,000 Japanese defenders survived this with scores of underground fortresses connected by 16 miles of tunnels stocked with
food, water, and ammunition. The surface was covered with concrete pillboxes and blockhouses housing some 800 gun positions.
On February 19, 1945, the attack began as the landing ships brought
the Marines towards the beaches of blackened volcanic sand.

Iwo Jima and Okinawa.

At 24, Sanford 'Sandy' Berkman was the old man of his outfit, serving as a second lieutenant in the 5th Division, 26th Marines, and wound up commanding a machine gun platoon on Iwo Jima. In 2007 he sat down for an interview with the New York State Military Museum's Veterans Oral History Project.

Sandy Berkman

We shoved off from Hawaii January 1, 1945, and we were part of an invasion force—not knowing where we were going at the time, but we found out later that we were going to Iwo. Everybody wanted to know where Iwo Jima was, no one had even heard of it. There had never been a white man on that island, only the Japanese—they owned and controlled it and lived there. We were aboard ship over forty days.

Arthur LaPorte was an eighteen–year-old Marine from Hudson Falls. He had been trained on the light machine gun in the 4th Marine Division. His convoy left training at Pearl Harbor for the long journey across the Pacific. It would be his first time in combat, as an ammunition carrier for a gun squad.

Art LaPorte

We went aboard ships right to Pearl [Harbor] and stayed at Pearl for a couple weeks until they got supplies and got the convoy together, and then we headed out, not knowing where we were going, across the Pacific on a huge convoy. We did not have any Japanese resistance; we were very lucky, no torpedoes or anything. We got out to Saipan and stayed offshore. After that, when we got going again, they brought out an easel, and they told us about how the Japanese had gun emplacements and what we would meet there. And that was our first knowledge that we were going to Iwo Jima.

We approached Iwo at night, and we could hear the gunfire from the ships. We could see the flashes and the firing, but we could not see Iwo at that time. Us new guys were too nervous to sleep, and we played poker all night. And even some of the old-timers, who were shaken up going into another battle, would be there with us.

Herb Altshuler joined the Marine Corps in April 1943 and was also assigned to the 4th Marine Division. The naval bombardment preceding the landings lasted three days.

Herb Altshuler

I remember very clearly how dramatic it was, seeing for the first time TV [monitors] with all these silhouetted ships and the beach.

It was quite an impressive thing going up on deck, and seeing as far as you could see, in a circle of 180 degrees, nothing but ships lined up. Battleships and destroyers and cruisers and all, just throwing in bombs right into this little island! You wondered how anybody would be there, how could anybody possibly live, and I think the leadership thought so too. They really thought they pulverized this island. It was amazing to see the armada of ships that were just lined up around this little island, just pounding it.

Sandy Berkman

We landed on Iwo February 19, 1945, and our division was part of the assault. Needless to say, it was a very, very tough operation, very costly in human lives. You couldn't move. It was all volcanic ash. We had poured some 18,000 rounds of [heavy] ammunition into the island from the battlewagons that were out there. And they [the Japanese] sat there and laughed at us; they were dug in. [Our] intelligence was not good—it later came out, and they admitted that it wasn't. We lost a lot of men. I lost a good deal of my platoon early.

Art LaPorte

Early in the morning, they fed us a steak dinner. Then we went up on deck, and we watched the 'goings-on' over Iwo. We looked out the stern of the ship, and there was Iwo standing right in front of us—Mount Suribachi to the left and a long stretch of beach, and to the right, some higher ground. The first outfit [went in] at 9:00. They hit the beaches, and we weren't scheduled to go in till the afternoon, but they lost so many men that we went in at 11:00. The thing that really got to us almost immediately—the boats were bringing back the wounded to our ship. I guess they were at least not-so-badly-hit casualties; the worst ones were being taken to the hospital ship. But they were bringing casualties back to our ship, and of course that made us quite nervous because we knew what we were getting into.

Herb Altshuler

I can remember very clearly watching the guys getting loaded onto the boats that were coming alongside and coming down the ladder, the netting. And I remember seeing a guy slip and getting crushed between the landing craft and the ship. I also remember very clearly that night when we had the burial at sea; we held service on deck, with a bugle and the works, and him being slipped over the side. Before you even went into battle, you were introduced to the reality of the war. I went in on the following day.

Art LaPorte

Our turn to hit the beach came at 11:00 a.m.; we were called in early. And the Japs didn't fire on us as we went in; I hardly saw any shells... When we got close to shore we were told to get in the landing craft. And when we landed at the beachhead, we ran out, and there was a slight rise ahead of us. It was hard to get over it because it was a mix of that black sand and volcanic ash and it was awful hard to get over it, and we were worried about the bullets.

Sandy Berkman

It was all volcanic ash; you couldn't dig. You'd dig a hole and it'd cave back in again. There was no such thing as digging a foxhole because it wouldn't hold. You lay there and hopefully you were all right. You see, they could see us, but we couldn't see them. They were so dug in, in these [fortified] emplacements. They had all those years to get that island ready, and especially when the war broke out, they knew that eventually we'd be going there. And they were waiting for us. There were over [20,000] of them. Probably, in the entire engagement, we landed over 40,000 men. You can imagine on an island [that small] with 60,000 men on there, it was just incredible. Absolutely incredible!

Herb Altshuler

Iwo was nothing but pulverized volcanic ash, and you sank in further over your ankles as you hit the beach. Now the Japanese had registered all their weaponry onto the beach, so you were there and you were just sitting ducks. The idea was to get in and get in as far as you could, and I remember doing that. And I remember that night, I crawled in a foxhole—well, actually, it was a hole that was caused by one of their large mortars. I had been lying there, and a 'recon' came by. A 'recon' was a small vehicle loaded with rockets, and it was dark, and it pulled up alongside of where I was, and I dug in, just holding onto my rifle, scared as hell, and he let go of all of his rockets, which flashed and made a big bright spot. After he let all of his rockets go he just drove off, and I thought, 'Well, this is the end.' These guys [the Japanese] would just register on me, but I was lucky that it didn't happen. I remember lying there thinking about all of the stuff I hadn't done [in my life]. Then I fell asleep.

"Trapped by Iwo's treacherous black-ash sands."
Mount Suribachi in background.
National Archives. Public domain.

Walter Hammer had just turned 21 a few months before the landing.

Walt Hammer

When we landed, our landing craft got hit. I was a heavy machine gunner carrying a 43-pound receiver [*the midsection 'business' action of the machine gun*]. We had a tripod carrier and also a guy who carried the barrel, which had a handle on it and a little pocket. Well, when we landed, I got ashore, and the landing craft backed off and the barrel went with it! Now we were ashore, so I said to Looney, 'We can't damn do anything right now, so take that tripod and put it on the ground, and let me put my receiver on there.' First thing that had to be done [on the beach] anyway was to start finding the mines, or we wouldn't have gotten any tanks, bulldozer tanks, or flamethrower tanks in there. So for a while, that's what we were doing...We were doing engineering work to make a pass up there [off the beach], putting the white tape on the side so that we could get the heavy equipment in. Later on, about two days later, the barrel showed up!

The Japanese were dug in and they had cisterns all over the island, and those got destroyed by our Navy [shelling]. The water ran out and a lot of those cisterns became operating rooms for the doctors. Doctors took those over. And the Japanese themselves, as this campaign wore on, they started wanting for water, so they used to go out and take the canteens from the dead Marines. They'd take their [empty] food cans and they'd set them outside so that when it did rain, they could collect the water. Now I understand that [the Japanese soldier] lived a miserable life underground, and he had to get the water so that he could take his biscuits and soak them so that he could eat them. And the lice drove 'em crazy! [*Laughing*] They lived that way, and they fought that way, and they fought to the very end. They stayed in the ground and they died in the ground.

At Iwo Jima, Ralph Leinoff made his fourth invasion landing as a Marine.

Ralph Leinoff

The first wave landed, they went ashore, and apparently there was very little resistance. They started to move inland and a few minutes later the second wave hit, and they started to move inland. And the wave I was in, the third one, we hit behind them and we started moving inland, and suddenly all hell broke loose!

We were sitting there on these open beaches. Our unit had to get up to this airfield, we wanted that airfield. When I went ashore, I had seven or eight men—the table of organization for a machine gun squad calls for eight men, but by the end of the first day, I had three guys left! I went in with seven, and I lost about half of them. Not killed, but so badly wounded that they couldn't go any further. And we were only about halfway up to the airfield and I tried to get up as far as I could [with the men]. Machine gun squads in an infantry company are in support of the riflemen. The riflemen are supposed to lead the way; the machine guns are supposed to protect them, set up crossfire in front of them, so that any enemy coming at us, the machine guns could take them out. When it became apparent that we had suffered so many casualties by the end of the first day, everybody just dug in where they were, halfway up to the landing field.

We got the word to stay where we were, we were in for the night, and we had to wait for reinforcements. When dusk came the Japanese couldn't see us that well, so the firing died down quite a bit. I said, 'We are going to dig in here tonight,' then I looked at one of my men, Tom Keiser from California, and I saw him up close for the first time that day. He had a big patch on his right cheek. I said, 'What happened to you, Tom?' He said, 'Nothing.' I said, 'I want to see what is under that patch, I don't know if you should be here.' Well, I made him take off the patch and I could see a piece of shrapnel and I think it went through, but I couldn't tell clearly because it was dusk and all. He took it off and I could see a pretty good gouge out of his cheek, and I said, 'Okay, Tom, you are out of it, you go back to the first aid. You have had enough.' He said he wasn't going. So we had an argument, again—before the landing, we had had an argument about some of the weaponry that I wanted the squad to carry. I said, 'Yesterday you wanted out of my squad, now I am telling you to go back! I don't need another wounded man on my hands! I will wait until I get relief in the morning!' He said to me, 'I am not leaving you with two men.'

What do you say to that? I was about 21; I did not know how to take it. I did not know if I should thank him, or tell him to follow orders, but I needed him. I really needed the manpower, and he says, 'I am not leaving you.' I was kind of flabbergasted. To make a long story short, Tom stayed with me for the rest of the war.

Art LaPorte

Our target was an airbase. They had one main airfield, and they had another smaller one, and the third one they were still working on. That was where I got wounded, the unfinished airfield. They had Mount Suribachi, the highest peak, which the 5th Division took. We had the next highest peak, which was Hill 382—you name them by height. The day I got hit, my company went against it. They lost half of the men and had to pull back.

Mount Suribachi was quite a sight, too. There, for a while, you could watch what was going on. They put spotlights on it at night, and they were pounding with everything they had! They put 20-mm and 5-inch guns—and the 16s—they were really pounding it. I don't know if it did any good, the [Japanese] had the caves. But they were really working it over!

Flag of our Fathers

AP combat photographer Joe Rosenthal took the iconic photo of the flag-raising on Iwo Jima. As at Peleliu, mission planners had expected the island to fall within a few days. Only a third of Iwo Jima had been taken when the U.S. flag appeared over the peak of Mount Suribachi on D–Day+4.

Art LaPorte

I didn't actually see the flag go up. We were pretty far inland, by that time, from the cliffs. I volunteered with another guy to go and get some food for the platoon. As we approached the cliffs, I looked over and I saw the flag flying. I said to my buddy—not knowing that it would become so famous—I said, 'What in the devil do they have that flying for? We haven't even taken this damned place...'

Sandy Berkman

I lasted four and a half days. I got hit on February 23, about 30 minutes after the flag went up on Suribachi. Part of my outfit went to Suribachi, and the rest of us went to the airfield. We had to secure the airfield—that's the way they broke us up.

By the fourth day we'd only advanced less than a mile. We were pinned down most of the time. We couldn't even set ourselves up to meet the enemy. I was lying there waiting to pull my platoon up into a flank, and I looked over and I saw the flag up, and it was a wonderful sight. I saw the first flag. There were two flags that went up. Then they put up the second flag—that was the famous photograph. About thirty minutes after that, I guess they [the Japanese] got a little mad at us, because we got everything thrown at us, and I got hit. I got hit with a mortar shell, all across my back. I had eight pieces [of shrapnel], they found out later, that hit me.

I gave myself a shot of morphine. The officers were allowed to carry it; we were the only ones that could take it with us. And I gave myself a shot to ease the pain up a little bit. The corpsmen saw me, and they came and got me, and they took me out on a stretcher and they took me down to the beach. Then I went to a hospital ship. From the hospital ship, I went to Saipan to a field hospital, and from Saipan I went to Hawaii to a field hospital. From Hawaii I went to

San Francisco, and from San Francisco I went to St. Albans in Long Island. They tried to get you as close to home as they could. I was at St. Albans until June of 1945.

I lost a lot of people who I knew, especially in my platoon. I later found out that we had almost 100 percent casualties in my platoon. It was just a devastating place to be. The island was nothing, really, but we had to get the airfields. There was no question whether we had to or didn't have to—we had to, because by the time we completed the engagement, the first [U.S.] planes that landed were hit, and they would have never made it back to Saipan.

Ralph Leinoff

Now we were about two miles up from Mount Suribachi, where the flag was raised. We were put into a reserve position until we could get manpower; other units took over the front line, and we were put on reserve. While I was up on the airfield, I could see the mountain; I thought I spotted a little fleck of color up there at the top. I was like, 'What the hell is that?'—because you were still seeing smoke coming up. We didn't think that they had gotten up there. And I borrowed one of the officer's field glasses, I took a look, and I said, 'Son of a gun, there's an American flag flying—they're up there!' But what happened was they bypassed a lot of pillboxes to get up there; they got up there as fast as they could. They took a tremendous beating going up, and they went by a lot of Japanese machine gunners and all.

In his enthusiasm to be a Marine, Ralph had joined up, although he was still technically a member of the New York State Guard. He recalled mail call on Iwo Jima.

Ralph Leinoff, 2013. Portrait by Erica Miller.
Courtesy of the <u>Saratogian.</u>
[Note his painting in background.)

They brought up some fresh food, water, and supplies, and even brought up mail. At about two weeks into the operation, one of the letters I got was a postcard from the New York State Guard, threatening me with a court-martial because I had been missing the drills. So I told my sergeant, I said, 'Sergeant, I'm sorry to tell you this but I have to get back. I'm missing the drills in the New York State Guard. They want me back there.' [*chuckling*] He said, 'Get back to your foxhole.' [*He laughs again*] So it was kind of a comical relief.

So anyway, we started to get mail, and one of the things I got that was distributed by the Navy was a small edition of *Time Magazine.* And as I sat there eating a sandwich I was going through this small magazine, and I came upon the picture, the [now famous] photograph—it was all black and white, no color. I said, 'Son of a—

look at this silhouette! There's six guys here trying to raise the flag on Mount Suribachi!' So I started drawing. We had nothing else to do; we were in reserve until we got up there to the airfield. I had letterhead, I had a pencil, and so on—I was drawing it! And I kept the drawing, and finally when we got back to our base in Maui, I was serious. I said, 'I'm going to go get some paper and some paint—some watercolors.' At that time it just came out, nobody really knew [how iconic the picture would become]. The paintings that the artists made afterward with the oil, of course, were much superior. I'm not a professional artist, but yes, I used to try to paint pictures of some of the men who were killed. I would try to make a picture and send it home to the family. I didn't do too many, because some of the letters I got back in appreciation were really heartbreaking...and they wanted to know the 'when, how, and why'; they wanted all the details, how the men got killed, and, well, it's... [*pauses a short while*] War is hell, it really is, and if you try to describe it, it just—it just can't be done, can't be done.

Art LaPorte

Art's unit moved up to secure the unfinished airfield. Looking for cover, he received a shock.

We got the word that one of our outfits got the pounding pretty bad, so we were the replacements. We went up during the night, early morning, and moved into position. They told us to get in a foxhole. I got into a foxhole quickly, and there was another Marine sitting there. I see his feet. I brought my eyes up his body, and his rifle was standing beside him. So I said to him, 'I'm going to get in with you, all right?' And no answer. As I come up his body, no head [*motions across his neck*]. Some Japanese officer or somebody with a sword had taken his head off during the night. I felt the hair raise on the back of my head, and I got away from there! I found another foxhole and jumped in it.

Art LaPorte.

'*I've got a good one for you, Doc.*'

That morning, 12 days into the attack, Art was hit.

I was kind of in a shallow place, I was going to run up and join my outfit—they were a little ahead. All of a sudden a sniper was putting shots right by my head. I could almost feel it, so I figured I better run. So I zigzagged. Of course, if you zigzag, you make yourself a harder target. Next thing I know, I'm flying through the air. A machine gun burst had gone by me, and they were using explosive bullets. And so, luckily, I landed in a 5-inch shell hole; our guns on the destroyers were 5 inches in diameter across the shell, like the battlewagons had 16-inch diameters across that shell. Now the 16-inch shell was about across-my-body wide [*motioning*], 2,000 pounds, and you can imagine what explosive that is. You could put about 15 or 20 people in the [crater made by the shell on impact],

I'd say. So I looked down at my leg, and I could see the bone, and you could put your fist into it. I could hear some guys in the next 16-inch shell hole, so I think I hollered over to them, 'I'm hit.' I wasn't feeling any pain, I was in shock. As bad as it is, it was no pain that I remember. And so, I heard somebody running, and somebody popped down on me, and the machine gun was trying to get him. And it was my sergeant, section leader. And he says, 'How bad you hit?' And I said, 'Pretty bad.' I think he said, 'Jesus,' and he ran into the 16-inch shell hole. And this time, another body landed on me, and it was a corpsman this time. And he tried to patch me up, but that machine gun kept trying to pick him off. So he says, 'I can't work on you here, I haven't got room enough,' because it was very shallow. And he said, 'Would you take a chance? We can push you across to the 16-inch shell hole.' It was a short distance, maybe 10 feet. I said, 'Sure, I got to get patched up.' So he pushed against my good leg, and I'm trying to crawl. And the other guys in the 16-inch shell hole are reaching out for me. And one of them got a graze against the wrist.

They got me down in the hole; it was pretty deep, probably six or eight feet deep. Quite wide, too. They worked on me—patched me up. Then they left; they had to go to Hill 382. So all day I was there, I tried to drink water. But I couldn't, I'd throw it up. Tried to eat food, same thing. I noticed a funny sensation, like something wet. I knew that they had bound up the wounds good. I was worried about hemorrhaging, so I pulled up my pants leg, and there was a fountain—about an inch or two high—coming out of my kneecap. A piece of shrapnel had gone in and hit an artery or whatever is in there. I had used my bandage on my wounds; the only thing I had was toilet paper. So I put that on with some pressure, and it stopped the bleeding.

I was by myself in the shell crater. I was all alone. All kinds of weapons were firing because they were trying to pick our men off.

My company was going against 382. And, of course, I was right in line with it. I'd peep up and try to see how they were doing, but I didn't dare to stand up on my good leg. I looked back toward some rocks behind me. Some of our men were there, and stretcher-bearers, but they didn't dare send anyone because there were so many bullets flying around. And they didn't want to lose four men to save one.[24]

I was there about eight hours. I was concerned that they would leave me there and the Japanese would get me. Then, my sergeant came by and asked if I was still there. I don't know how he got me out of that 16-inch shell hole but he asked me if I could stand on the good leg. He put me in a fireman's carry and carried me out under fire.

On the hospital ship, LaPorte waited his turn for surgery.

From where I was I could watch the doctors operate. It was a table, and around the table was a trough. What fascinated me was when the trough was filled with blood, and when the ship would rock, the blood would go back and forth in unison with the ship.

They finally got to me, and I believe I said to the doctor, 'I've got a good one for you, Doc.' Because the one that was ahead of me apparently couldn't take the pain too good. And he was screaming and hollering, and I could see the doctor. They were working right around the clock, and they looked awful tired. And I said to myself, 'I'm not going to give them a hard time'—they had enough trouble. So when he got to me, I watched him. It really didn't bother me. I could see him clipping with scissors around the wound, taking the jagged edges off. Then, when I got done, they put me out on the

---

[24] As on Peleliu and in other battles, the Japanese would target corpsmen and stretcher-bearers.

side where I could look out and see Iwo. Like a sundeck or something. That was the last time I saw Iwo—we sailed for Guam.

The Guys Left Behind

Herb Altshuler

One thing I will always remember is the day or two before we left the island, before we got back on that ship, they had services and they dedicated the cemetery on Iwo. I remember sitting on a hill looking down and there was a flag pole—they used dogs for bringing messages back from the front forward to the firing units in the back, and they had the [dead] dogs lined up around the flagpole where they were to be buried... You see a large area of your [dead] men just lined up, and... then I saw heavy equipment, and that [the ground] was plowed, and all the dead bodies were laid out. You could see dead bodies as far as you wanted to look, and then you realized that war was not fun and games. These were the guys that were left behind.

A total of 27 Medals of Honor were awarded for individual acts of heroism under fire at Iwo Jima. The island was deemed secure on March 25—25 days longer than planners had counted on. Nearly 7,000 Americans and 19,000 Japanese died at Iwo Jima. It was the Marines' costliest battle ever.[42]

CHAPTER ELEVEN

Captivity-Year 4:
The Copper Mine

As 1945 dawned, Joe Minder and 500 other prisoners would depart from Formosa for the Japanese home islands. After nearly two weeks, they arrived in Kyushu, where they would then be shipped north in boxcars to arrive at a freezing copper mine, slaving for Japanese industrialists. Many of the major Japanese corporations lobbied the government intensively for the opportunity to exploit American laborers, especially skilled ones, though the prisoners were routinely starved and abused. Nearly forty percent of the 27,000 American slave laborers died in captivity.[25] Joe's journey was far from over.

---

[25] U.S. Congressional Research Service. To date, out of the 60 Japanese corporations that profited from American slave labor during the war, just one has formally apologized. Said one daughter: 'This isn't going to end even when all of the former POWs pass away. Their children and grandchildren have heard and lived with the stories, and they haven't forgotten. This isn't about money. It's about acknowledging what was done to these men.' [time.com/3334677/pow-world-war-two-usa-japan]

Joe Minder

Hell, Revisited

January 12, 1945

Hell again! Found out last night that we're going to be shipped to Japan.

Americans are much more active around here now. We have seen many planes fly over our camp and have also heard the rumble of bombs and strafing from the Yank planes. I hate to think of dodging those torpedoes and bombs on the open seas again, but God saved us on that last trip and if he answers our prayers, we will make this okay, also.

4:00 p.m.

Arrived at Port Takao by train and went aboard a little larger ship this time, named *Melbourne Maru*. After loading on sugar and salt, we sailed for Moji, Japan.

January 22, 1945

We didn't have contact with any Yanks until today when we had another attack by an American sub. Several depth charges were dropped and drove it off. Now we are wondering if American planes will be after us!

January 23, 1945

Sailed safely into Moji.

January 25, 1945

Disembarked at Moji, got on train and started for Hanaoka on the northern tip of Japan.

January 29, 1945

After a four-day bitter-cold train ride, we finally arrived here at camp, where we will work in this open copper mine as soon as a little of this snow melts. What a different climate—in the south of Japan there are oranges on the trees, here there is about four feet of snow and it is cold as heck!

Mittens Made of Grass

February 20, 1945

Started working in the mine today, loading dirt into four-wheeled steel cars and pushing them about one mile by hand. With only shoes and mittens made of grass, our hands and feet are about to freeze in this bitter cold!

March 6, 1945

Had our first bath in 54 days today! They broke down and even gave us wood to heat our water with!

What a camp this is! We have to carry all water from outside the camp and carry the wood in on our backs, about two miles from here. They ration the wood out to us every day. Those 15 sticks which they give us don't even take the chill off of our barracks. Several men are suffering from chilled feet and hands.

April 1, 1945

One hundred men arrived in camp from Kawasaki.

April 4, 1945

Received one American Red Cross food parcel per man. I enjoyed this better than any other chow that I have ate in my life!

April 19, 1945

Received second Red Cross parcel, less a half can of butter, due to stealing by new men in camp.

May 5, 1945

Celebrated my birthday by having a can of pâté baked into a rice loaf. Also had some coffee, which I saved from my Red Cross parcel.

June 18, 1945

Four men escaped from camp!

Working conditions are steadily getting harder and our food is getting lousier every day. When we first got here, we received a little fish and horse bones to flavor our soup, but we have to work on plain watery greens soup and a small bowl of barley.

Several men have gotten so weak out in the mine that they have fainted and tumbled off of the ledges while picking at the dirt!

June 28, 1945

Our morale went up today when 45 Australian officers joined our camp! They gave us the dope as to how the Yanks were blasting Tokyo and other large cities south of here. Where their camp was located in southern Japan, bombing became so terrific that the Japs were forced to evacuate the entire area!

CHAPTER TWELVE

A Rain of Ruin

Strategic bombing raids to Japan began in earnest from the newly liberated Mariana Islands as the fighting ended in the early summer of 1944. By early 1945, wave after wave of the sleek new B–29 Superfortresses began to arrive in the skies over Japan. A quantum leap in aviation technology, the B–29 was much longer, wider, and faster than its predecessor, the B–17, and capable of carrying a much larger bomb load over vast expanses of ocean over thousands of miles. Additionally, the densely populated industrial areas of Japan and the dispersal of Japanese industry into domestic settings (i.e., people's homes) would have grave consequences for the populations within the areas to be targeted.

The coupling of the B–29 with the development and deployment of incendiary "firesticks," six-pound cylinders filled with napalm, or gelatinized gasoline, was a very serious development for the enemy, indeed. While few were willing to face up to the inevitable, the death and destruction brought by the B–29s would plunge the country into a feeling that it had never felt before in its thousand-year history: a mixture of desperation and quiet despair.[43]

Andy Doty, a 1943 graduate of Hudson Falls High, was tasked as a tail gunner on 21 combat missions in the B–29 in the skies over the vast Pacific in these raids on the Japanese home islands. Landing in Guam for the first time as part of an eleven-man crew, he recounted his first missions and the horrors of war as witnessed by a twenty-one–year-old kid from Hometown, USA.

Andy Doty

My earliest impressions of our new home were of jungle, rain, and mud. We lived in tents surrounded by high rows of uprooted trees and got about on wooden walkways. After a few weeks we moved into newly constructed Quonset huts that were high and dry.

Not long after we arrived, the pilot and co-pilot went on a mission to Japan as observers. They were strangely noncommittal when they came back.

'What was it like?' I asked the lieutenant, our co-pilot, a day later.

'It was interesting. Spectacular. You'll find out soon enough.'

The First Mission

Our turn came not long afterward. On March 30 we were alerted for our first raid. We made our way to the briefing tent that was filled with combat crews sprawled on rows of benches. At the front was a huge map. The Marianas were at the bottom. Iwo Jima was halfway up, and the Japanese homeland angled across the top, 1,600 miles away.

A red string led from our base straight to Nagoya, on the main island of Honshu. It was to be a high altitude daylight mission against the Mitsubishi aircraft engine factory, one of the two largest engine plants in Japan. It was a heavily defended target that previous missions had failed to destroy. Briefing officers told us about the importance of the complex. We listened closely to reports about the weather, the location of enemy anti-aircraft batteries, the positions of rescue submarines and aircraft, the tactics of Japanese fighter planes, and other details. A chaplain concluded the session with a short prayer. We sat with heads bowed.

We gathered up our parachute harnesses, parachutes, inflatable 'Mae West' life preservers, survival vests, helmets, oxygen masks, hunting knives, sunglasses, and other items, and climbed into a truck with benches along each side. There was little talk in the darkness as we rode to our hardstand.

Much to our disappointment, the new bomber we had flown to Guam had been taken away from us and assigned to a more veteran crew. We inherited an older plane, No. 43 92996, and unloaded in front of it. We climbed aboard to check our equipment and positions, then returned to sit on the pavement near the front landing gear, our backs against the big wheels.

A long hour later, it was time to go. We paired up to pull the big propeller blades down and through, twelve turns per blade, to make certain that no oil had accumulated in the lower cylinder heads. I climbed up the rear ladder and started the auxiliary generator.

'Putt-putt started and on line,' I reported.

'Roger,' the pilot, our captain, replied. The men up front closed the bomb bays and switched on the first engine. The propellers slowly began to turn. The engine coughed to life, spewed smoke, and settled into a steady roar. Three other engines followed in turn.

Into the Air

Few wartime scenes can be more dramatic than dozens of heavy bombers departing on a mission. I will never forget the sight. One at a time, on a precise schedule, the B–29s inched out of their paved revetments and fell into line, brakes screeching, high tails bobbing in the moonlight like some prehistoric monsters. Nose to tail, the bombers edged ahead in a slow parade to the head of the runway. The air was filled with noise and fumes.

The large flaps at the back edge of our wings were slowly extended as we moved ahead, adding a fifth more surface area to the bomber's narrow wings. The flaps allowed take-offs and landings at lower speeds.

'Left flap, twenty-five degrees,' the waist gunner reported to the pilot. 'Right flap, twenty-five degrees,' the opposite waist gunner added.

A wooden control tower lay ahead, to the right of the runway. Red and green lights from the tower triggered a take-off every minute. When the green light flashed, the captain opened the engines to full power and stood on the brakes, holding us fast as the engines roared. He released the brakes, and we began lumbering down the long runway. It was a dangerous moment, with little margin of safety; the temperamental engines had to haul a thirty–five-ton bomber, four tons of bombs, eight thousand gallons of gasoline, thousands of rounds of ammunition, and eleven men into the air.

We slowly picked up speed, engines roaring, wisps of vapor trailing from open engine cowlings that reminded me of the laid back ears of a running dog. We seemed to hug the ground forever. The captain held the nose down to gain as much speed as possible, then eased us into the air. He touched the brakes briefly to stop the wheels from spinning once we were airborne.

The lieutenant quickly retracted the wheels into the inboard engine nacelles [housings] to rid ourselves of the air resistance. 'Gear up,' he said. We sagged over the rocky headlands at the end of the island, adding speed as we dropped. The captain 'milked' the flaps back into the wings as we sped on.

Seated in the tail, I watched the bombers behind us, the runway, the cliffs, and the island disappear. We were on our way. After a time I test fired my guns, went back through the unpressurized section to turn off the 'putt-putt,' and joined the others in the waist compartment for the long trip. We had left at three in the morning to reach our target seven hours later. That timing would give us several hours of daylight for our return to Guam after the bomb run.

Three and one half hours later we passed over Iwo Jima, a brown pork chop-shaped island halfway to Japan. Marines had taken it from the Japanese only a few days earlier after a monumental battle. The island's new landing strip, built while the fighting still raged, already was a welcome haven for bombers in distress.

Although the B-29's top speed was 358 miles an hour, it actually was flown more slowly when loaded with bombs and gas, and when a long trip lay ahead. The average indicated airspeed was closer to 220 miles an hour, which meant that the crews had to spend more than fifteen and one half hours in the air on every mission. The trip from Guam to Japan and back covered some 3,200 miles.

Three hours after we passed over Iwo, the captain announced that he was starting the climb to our bombing altitude of 25,000 feet. I returned to the tail and settled in. Ahead of us a lead bomber, its nose wheel extended for identification, circled above a tiny volcanic island off the coast of Japan. Arriving B-29s cut across the wide circle to catch up to the leader and other bombers. We edged into a formation of twelve planes. Once we had assembled we joined 256 Superforts in a long bomber stream, headed for Nagoya.

B–29s over Mt. Fuji, 1945. USAAF. Public domain.

The Bomb Run

The side windows of my tail compartment flared out slightly. I could crane my head around to see the wings and engines. Looking down, I saw the coast of Japan appear beneath a wing. The enemy territory appeared dark and foreboding. There was no turning back. We were being drawn inexorably toward a point high in the sky above Japan's second largest city.

My stomach was tight as we continued on and turned into our bomb run. We were flying in close formation, keeping each other company as we maximized our fire power and bombing pattern. One B–29 was just behind and below our plane, only yards away. I looked into the front cabin, where the bombardier, pilot, and copilot were hunched tensely in their flak suits, oxygen masks, and helmets.

I kept my guns angled straight up in the air, knowing that the men in the following bombers were frightened by friendly weapons pointed in their direction.

It was quiet in our bomber as we bore ahead in perfect weather. The first puffs of anti-aircraft fire began to appear. I strained to watch in every direction for enemy aircraft.

'Twelve o'clock level,' the lieutenant shouted, and the guns chattered up front. A Japanese fighter flashed through our formation, the pilot's head swiveling as he looked about. I fired as soon as I could without hitting any bombers behind us. Someone had hit him—I hadn't—and he bailed out. He drifted to earth far to the rear.

As we neared the target area, the anti-aircraft fire increased. Our introduction to the war was a sky filled with ugly black bursts of fire, each burst sending jagged bits of steel flying in all directions.

I tried to shrink my body into the smallest possible target. The deadly puffs contrasted with the long, almost beautiful white tentacles of phosphorous bombs that were dropped into our formation by a Japanese plane flying above us. It was a surrealistic scene. Several bursts walked silently in a line toward our plane, but stopped short. Out of range to our right, a twin-engine Japanese fighter radioed our speed and altitude to the ground batteries.

I was struck by the unreality of it all, although nothing could be more real. Perhaps all warriors are somewhat traumatized by their situations. We were in the thick of it, five miles above Japan, and yet I was observing myself and our situation almost with detachment. The cool interior of my compartment, the gleaming bombers all about us, the clear air outside, the vicious bursts of flak, the masked and helmeted men huddled in the plane close behind, all seemed from another world.

We were suspended in time on a steady bomb run from which we could not deviate. Flak described as 'intense and accurate' crashed all about us. Finally our bombardier called out 'bombs away' and our plane surged upward, relieved of its burden. Looking around, I saw schools of fat, 500-pound bombs drop from the other bombers and begin their long slants to earth; looking down moments later, I could see explosions twinkling in the target area, much like strings of tiny Chinese firecrackers.

Our formation wheeled into a long turn to head back home. Off the coast, the individual bombers spread out to begin their solitary flights to Guam. The feeling of relief in our B–29 was palpable.

'My,' the left waist gunner said. 'That was quite a party!'

'Only thirty-four more to go,' the radioman added. No one answered.

Post-strike photos showed 'excellent' results; *The New York Times* reported the next day that the target had been hit squarely by our bombs, resulting in the 'virtually total destruction of the vast works.' All but twenty-four of the 140 buildings were destroyed, some 3,446,000 square feet of roof space.

The anti-aircraft fire was 'the heaviest yet encountered,' according to the reports of veteran crew members, and fighter opposition was severe. Five aircraft were lost and more than half the bombers were damaged by flak, but I did not see any Superforts go down.

'Look what you did to my airplane!' our ground crew chief said after we landed and returned to our revetment. He mounted a ladder to poke the end of a screwdriver into one of the small holes that had been created by bits of flak on the underside of our right wing.

'Sorry about that,' said the captain.

Perdition

If the bombing run over Nagoya seemed interminable, the next one seemed even longer. It came over Tokyo on April 13, during the second low-level incendiary raid on that city.

Although our high-altitude Nagoya mission had been successful, earlier precision bombing from that height had been largely ineffective because of the dense clouds and strong winds above Japan. Clear weather was found over the target only four to seven days a month. General Curtis LeMay, head of the 20th Air Force, concluded that individual B-29s, flying in at 5,000 to 8,000 feet at night, would be far more accurate than if they bombed from 25,000 to 30,000 feet. They could burn out large areas of the Japanese cities, 'de-house' the population, and destroy the many cottage industries that supported the war effort.

Another major advantage was that the bombers would not have to make the long, demanding climb to high altitudes that strained the engines and drank up fuel. Nor would they have to assemble in formation and jockey about on the way to the target. Consequently, they could carry twice the bomb load. Engine maintenance would be reduced, which would result in more bombers over the target.

LeMay's decision had dismayed the B–29 crews. The low-level raids obviously were much closer to ground anti-aircraft and searchlight batteries, and left less room for crewmen to bail out if their plane was shot down. Many B–29s were seen to catch fire, explode, and plunge to earth. The incendiary raids against major cities were not welcomed by the airmen.

We took off late in the afternoon on a mission appropriately code named 'Perdition'—hell, utter destruction, entire loss, ruin. Our target was the arsenal area of the city, six miles northwest of the Imperial Palace. It was a sector that contained housing and factories that made or stored machine guns, artillery, bombs, and other arms. An estimated 30,000 to 80,000 people lived in every square mile of that area.

Each of the 348 bombers carried between five and eight tons of incendiary bombs, depending upon the distance they had to fly. Guam was 125 miles south of Saipan, so our ground crew loaded fewer bombs and more fuel. Each of our main bombs contained a cluster of fifty–five smaller bombs filled with jellied gasoline; the big bombs opened at 5,000 feet to scatter the smaller ones. One bomber could create a flaming swath a half–mile wide and a mile and a half long.

The Death of the President

As we flew north that night, we heard on our headsets that President Roosevelt had died suddenly while vacationing in Georgia. The news shocked us, for we were fond of our president and respected his steady leadership. We buzzed about the development for a time, speculating about the little known vice president, Harry Truman, who now would move into the White House. We put the news behind us and concentrated again on the mission ahead.

Inferno

We arrived off the coast at midnight. Looking ahead, I could see the glow of the burning city. We had heard about the three hundred anti-aircraft guns awaiting us, and were fearful. The report was that bombers caught in the searchlight beams above the city often were goners.

'This is it,' someone said as we bore ahead.

'Stay off the intercom,' the captain ordered.

Once over the city, I looked down into an indescribable scene. Tokyo was an inferno. Block after block of buildings were aflame. The fire covered eleven square miles of the city, and smoke towered thousands of feet into the air. The smell of burning wood and other materials came through our open bomb bays. A violent updraft suddenly drove us hundreds of feet higher, pinning us to our seats. I could hardly lift my hand.

Searchlights swept the sky and tracer fire laced through the night. I strained to watch for other bombers and Japanese night fighters. A few thousand feet above us, and to the rear, I saw a silver bomber caught by the searchlight beams. It shone brightly in the night sky. Bombs began tumbling down from its open bays, shimmering in the light of the fires and the beams.

Suddenly a beam fastened on our own bomber, and it was quickly joined by others. It was bright enough inside my compartment to read a newspaper. I felt naked in the grip of the beams as we plunged wildly ahead, waiting for our load of bombs to be dropped. They finally fell free, and the captain nosed the plane down to gain speed.

'Let's get the hell out of here!' he said as he banked swiftly down and away. We were greatly relieved as we headed home. More than one hundred miles from the city, I could still see the red glow in the sky. Beneath that glow, thousands of people were dead or dying.

Some 2,100 tons of bombs fell on Tokyo that night. *B–29s Set Great Tokyo Fires; Explosions Heard 100 Miles,'* the *Times* reported afterward. A correspondent who flew in a 314th Wing bomber wrote:

'A very large task force of B-29s swarmed over Tokyo, a minute apart, in the darkness early today with millions of pounds of incendiaries. From my vantage point in this battleship of the sky, it appeared that the Army Air Force had achieved its goal of wiping out the fire-able sections of the Japanese capital. The sight of the capital aflame would thrill any American, and it was especially exciting for me, marking my first combat mission in the Pacific air theater.'

Seven bombers and seventy–seven men failed to return. Our crew had emerged shaken, but unscathed.

The 15th Mission

I wrote home to my parents before our fifteenth mission. 'This should all be over pretty soon,' I said. 'The Japs can't keep it up. They're running out of gas.'

We took off for Osaka early in the morning of June 7. Our regular radar man was ill, and was replaced by a young radar officer. He was quiet on our flight north, a handsome fellow among strangers, intent on the green radar screen in his dark room.

We were fairly confident it would be an easy run, for we had seen few fighters in recent weeks and the anti-aircraft fire was growing weaker. The flight was even easier than we expected; all of Japan was blanketed by heavy clouds. We saw no land from the time we neared the coast until we left it. We bombed by radar and saw only a few bursts of flak well away from our bomber.

A hundred miles off the coast on our way home, we began to relax. I was still watching behind us when something caught my eye. Far to the rear, to my lower right, a twin-engine fighter plane popped up above the clouds, and then dropped down. He was on the prowl, hoping to catch us by surprise.

'Tail to crew,' I called out. 'A fighter just came out of the clouds at seven o'clock low and dropped back down. Get ready.'

It was an Irving, the name that had been given to a night fighter that was equipped with radar and heavy armament. I entered his wingspan into my gun sight and waited. The black plane suddenly emerged a few thousand yards to the rear, climbing rapidly at my lower left.

'Five o'clock low,' I cried out, and found him in my sight. I narrowed the circle of dots down to his wing tips, and began squeezing off bursts. He opened fire at the same time. The machine guns in his wings flared again and again as he closed in. His glowing tracer bullets flew lazily by, looking almost harmless. He kept coming until he was a few hundred yards away. The image of that black fighter, his winking guns, and the slow motion tracers will stay with me forever.

I slowly opened the ring to hold it around his wing tips, and continued firing. I was aware that I was spacing my bursts, letting up for a few seconds as he bore in. My bullets were striking his right engine, sending parts flying. Smoke began pouring from the engine, and the pilot broke off his attack. He banked down into the clouds, a long, black plume trailing behind. I have often wondered if he made it home safely, and where he is today. One of his engines was still operating, so he probably was able to return to his base.

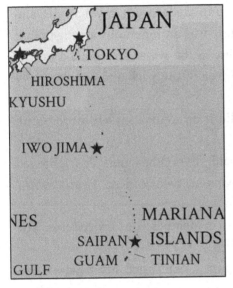

Late that day, as we were nearing home, I became aware that something was wrong. The captain and our flight engineer were talking about headwinds and the amount of fuel that remained in our wing tanks, as they so often did. But this time I could tell they were worried. Finally the flight engineer said, 'It's going to be close.'

Not long after, the captain came onto the intercom.

'We've got a little problem up here,' he said. 'We've hit some headwinds, and might not be able to make it back. Y'all should get ready, in case we have to ditch or bail out.'

By that time, we were well south of Saipan and forty-five miles north of Guam. So not only the Japanese were running out of gas. I scrambled quickly back to the tail, where my life raft rested in its canvas pack within the seat frame. I snapped my chest parachute onto my harness. Listening from the tail, I could hear that the situation was worsening.

I lifted out the life raft pack and attached it to the rings on the bottom of my parachute harness. A long strap hung from the raft inside the pack. I pulled the strap underneath my harness and snapped it onto my Mae West. It was an ingenious arrangement; once I shucked the chute harness in the water and yanked on the strap, the raft would be pulled free of the pack and automatically inflate.

I folded my seat back and slid it up to give myself more room. The intercom clicked.

'No time left', the captain said. 'Everybody out!' A frightened voice broke in. It was the replacement radar officer. 'I can't swim,' he cried out. 'I can't swim!'

'You don't have to,' I said. 'Just remember your procedures. The life vest and raft should be enough.'

The bailout bell began ringing. I unplugged my headset, unsnapped my throat microphone, and opened the escape window. The air whipped by in a fearsome roar. As I moved to dive out, I found I could not; I was caught by the life raft strap, which had become snagged in the folded seat. I felt a wave of panic, and began tugging desperately at the strap. It would not come loose. The bell kept ringing. I thought of cutting the strap with my knife, but told myself to calm down to work the strap free. I unfolded the seat, slid it back down, and released the strap. I pushed the seat up, and went out the window.

Into the Ocean

First there was a rush and roar of air, then I tumbled over and over. Suddenly the parachute opened above me with a 'pop' and I was jerked to a halt. I have no memory of pulling the ripcord handle, or where it went afterward. My helmet was gone. It was strangely quiet except for the hum of our disappearing bomber. The evening sky was still pink from the sunset as I floated down.

I could see another chute against the black sea below, and called out to its owner. I undid my chest and leg straps and inflated my Mae West so that I could get out of the harness as quickly as possible after landing. I dangled there like a kid on a swing. As I watched, the horizon quickly closed in. For the first time, I realized that I would be alone in the ocean. I landed with a hard splash on my back and sank far deeper into the water than I ever imagined. It seemed a long time before I came up to the surface, even with an inflated vest. But I kept my mouth closed and held my breath until I surfaced. I threw off the parachute harness and pulled the life raft strap. The raft came out of its pack, and a gas cylinder opened it with a 'whoosh.' I drew the small raft to me and climbed in.

The waves were rolling monsters, flecks of white spray whipping from their crests. I rode them up and down as if on a roller coaster. Even when I was carried high on a wave, I saw no other crew members. I spent the night trying to sleep, being tipped over by the big swells, climbing back into the raft, and drying off only to be tipped over again. I was glad I had not cut the strap, for it kept the raft from blowing away when I was spilled into the water. Each time I was dumped into the sea, I thought about the possibility of sharks being in the area and scrambled back into the raft as quickly as I could.

A squall moved in. I collected rain in the rubber raft cover, washed the salt away as best I could, and drank all I could hold. I did not know how long it would be until help arrived.

Just before dawn, I noticed a dark shape in the distance. For a time I thought it was Rota, a small, Japanese-held island just north of Guam that had been bypassed [by our forces]. I did not want to be washed ashore, for B–29s that had to abort their missions dumped their bombs there before returning to Guam. The soldiers were not likely to be kind. I reversed the yellow side of the cover to the dark blue side and snuggled down even lower in the raft.

After a time, I heard the muffled chugging of an engine. The dark shape was a merchant ship that was looking for us. A search-light swept the ocean. 'Ship ahoy,' I called out, as they did in the movies. The beam came my way, and I waved my arms. It lighted on me. Soon the side of the ship loomed high above. A sailor came down a cargo net, grabbed my hand, and helped me out of the raft. I scrambled up the side, only to find my legs weak when I climbed over the railing and stood on the deck. Members of the ship's crew stood watching the strange scene. I was led below, given a hot shower, a shot of whiskey, an officer's underwear and bunk, and fell asleep.

Our waist gunners were picked up before I was. One said later that someone told him that another member of the crew had been found, and that 'he came up the side of the ship like a monkey.'

'That must be our tail gunner,' he said.

Three other members of the crew were not as fortunate. Our navigator and the flight engineer failed to open their life rafts and had drowned. They were found floating in their life vests, unable to keep their heads out of the choppy waves all night. Our radioman was able to do that; he did not get his raft open, but he fought to keep his head up. His neck was scraped raw by his life vest, but he survived.

I assumed that the replacement radar man who could not swim had leaped from the plane after I did. In the most bizarre aspect of the entire tragedy, I did not learn otherwise for many years. In actuality, he had gone down with the plane, refusing to jump despite the pleas of the waist gunners and our central fire control gunner. They considered throwing him out the rear door, but the central fire control gunner thought he could persuade him to jump by himself. He argued as long as he could, and then had to leap before it was too late. The radar man preferred to die in a crash rather than risk drowning in the sea.

The Unwritten Rule

They never talked about those awful moments, nor did I ever ask about them. Their need to deny or forget was complete, and I must have undergone the same subconscious process. It was only after I was reunited with one of the waist gunners, Jim Dudley, forty-five years after the war, that I learned the true story.

We could only speculate on what had happened to our navigator and flight engineer; possibly they had left their rafts behind. Possibly they had forgotten to attach the raft straps to their life vests, or had attached their straps over their chute harnesses instead of underneath them. Nor did we ever find out why we had not stopped at Iwo, Tinian, or Saipan to refuel. There was an unspoken agreement that the enlisted men should not press the captain too much on the subject, so we did not. We knew our place, and stuck to it.

My impression was that the captain disliked the long fueling delays, and enjoyed the attention that early arrivals from a mission received. He may have been eager to get back to report that we had beaten off an enemy fighter at a time when few were left in the skies. Whatever the reason, three young men paid with their lives.

Our encounter with the Irving was never reported; the damage inflicted on a Japanese fighter was incidental in light of what had happened to our bomber and the three men. I have since wondered if other B–29s that mysteriously disappeared off the coast of Japan without a trace during the war had fallen victim to surprise attacks such as ours.

A few days later we gathered at a military cemetery outside of Agana. The burial ground was located on a hillside, overlooking the Pacific. The sun was shining, a light breeze was blowing, and clouds were piled high in the sky. It was a glorious summer day. Our lives were continuing on; three others had come to an end.

An olive-drab Army ambulance with a large red cross arrived, bearing the remains of our navigator and flight engineer in wooden coffins with rope handles. I wondered where the radar man's body was. Thinking that he also had drowned, I assumed he was to be buried by members of his own crew at another time.

We opened the rear doors of the ambulance and slid the flight engineer's coffin toward us. As we did, the box tilted, and blood trickled from a crack onto the ground. The officers bore our navigator to his open grave as we carried our flight engineer to his. The graves were located side by side, approximating the way the two men had sat across an aisle from each other for hundreds of hours in the air. After an Air Force chaplain performed the funeral service, our central fire control gunner stepped up to the graves and wailed a Hebrew funeral chant. It was one of the saddest refrains I had ever heard. None of us dared look at the others. Our crew was sent on a one-week rest leave in Hawaii. Still stunned, we flew back in a comfortable Navy Douglas C-54 passenger plane. Seated close together on the long flight, we did not discuss what had happened. We dealt with our emotions by avoiding the incident altogether. Just as it was an unwritten rule not to question our captain, so it was that we did not revisit our experience. We were glad to be alive.

The Morality of War

Over sixty Japanese cities had been incinerated by the B–29s. Howling firestorms devoured civilians and workers in sheets of flames, burning hundreds of thousands to death.

When asked after the war about the morality of his orders to the crews of the B–29s, General LeMay responded, 'We knew we were going to kill a lot of women and children when we burned [Tokyo]... Killing Japanese didn't bother me much at the time. It was getting the war over with that bothered me.'

'We had to kill in order to end the war,' one pilot remembered. 'We heard about the thousands of people we killed, the Japanese wives, the children, and the elderly. That was war. But I know every B–29 air crewman for the next two or three years would wake up at night and start shaking. Yes, [the raids] were successful, but horribly so.'[44]

Aftermath of March 9–10, 1945 Tokyo raid. Ishikawa Kouyou.

While the population reeled and staggered, the Japanese High Command showed no signs of giving up the fight.

It would go on.

CHAPTER THIRTEEN

The Kamikazes

'People of the Philippines, I have returned... Rally to me. Let the indomitable spirit of Bataan and Corregidor lead on! As the lines of battle roll forward to bring you within the zone of operations, rise and strike![45]

On October 20, 1944, after three years of Japanese conquest and occupation, General Douglas MacArthur dramatically strode forth through the surf to arrive in the Philippines from Australia. The campaign for the liberation of Manila and the rescue of the prisoners, many of whom had felt abandoned by his abrupt departure two and a half years earlier, began even before Peleliu Island was secured. On the first day, more men would land at Leyte than the numbers put ashore that previous June to invade 'Fortress Europe' at Normandy on D-Day.[46]

Alvin Peachman was part of the naval force that put 200,000-plus American liberators ashore, and would also be a part of the Battle of Leyte Gulf, in which the Japanese Navy set into motion a complex 'oceanic banzai charge' to destroy the landing fleet and isolate the Americans now on land.[47]

Alvin Peachman

On the destroyer escort *USS Witter,* we made another trip to Saipan, and I got off there for a night. The captain was a good guy, because I had a brother there in the Army crew, and I asked if I could visit the Army anti-aircraft crew where he was. He said, 'Yeah, take the night off,' which I did. He was a good fellow. I went up there with the soldiers for a night with my brother.

Then we left there and October 1944 we made a lot of fleet exercises, and we invaded Leyte in the Philippine Islands. We carried in a bunch of soldiers there and I witnessed the battle both on land and later on the sea, because the Japanese closed in on us. We picked up and escorted several ships filled with ammunition, and several with fuel oil. We were under great aerial attack coming in and out. We got through and brought them to the fleet and they unloaded them in great haste to get ready for the Japanese Navy.

The Japanese Navy was converging from three different directions to take the gamble at destroying the invasion fleet.

Crossing the 'T'

Admiral Oldendorf was there with the 7th Fleet and crossed the 'T' on them and sank the whole Japanese fleet. They had to come up for what was called the Surigao Strait, which was a strait between Samar and Leyte. Every ship coming in in that division, in that area, was sunk.

'Crossing the T*' was the ideal in classical naval warfare. The battle line of the enemy's ships steams ahead in single 'vertical' file just as its attackers cross the top of the line horizontally, the bar of the 'T' allowing all of its broadside guns to be brought to bear while the enemy can only fire its forward-facing guns.*[48]

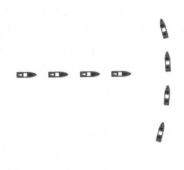

That didn't occur in other places. The Japanese Navy never attacked one spot. One of their fleets came through the center and Admiral Halsey had left that area, exposing our DEs [*destroyer escorts*] and light carriers, which we provided in force for Leyte, and it almost upset the whole invasion! He had gone further north, hunting the Japanese carriers; the Japanese had provided the bait for him to do that very thing!

The Japanese are not dumb people. Not only are they clever, but they are very brave and very fanatical. Every island we invaded had very few prisoners taken; they fought right to the last man. If they would have had our resources, it might have been a different story.

We then left that area because we were needed elsewhere. Before the rest of the Philippines were invaded, we went back down to New Guinea and we got ourselves ready there.

The greatest naval battle of the entire war had cost the Japanese nearly all of its Imperial Navy. However, at the conclusion of the three-day Battle of Leyte Gulf, a sinister new development began to harry the weary American crews. Out of the skies came suicide planes, armed with bombs, often closing on a target in pairs, intent on crashing into ships. The kamikazes, or 'divine wind,' took their inspiration from the typhoons which had saved Japan from Mongol invasions centuries before.

Back on land, 65,000 Japanese soldiers were killed at Leyte, with over 15,000 American casualties. The worst scenes of urban fighting in the Pacific took place for Manila, where in the month preceding February 1945, over 100,000 Filipino civilians died at the hands of the Japanese. The battles in the Philippines lasted until June 30, 1945. By this time, Alvin and the crew of the Witter were conducting tactical exercises and escort duties in the run-up to the massive Okinawa campaign, which would prove to be the last great amphibious operation of World War II.

Ulithi

Then we set sail for Ulithi. Ulithi Atoll was known as 'Shangri-La' to us, because it's a deep-water lagoon in the Carolines [where sailors could rest, swim, and get beer]. The Caroline Islands cover an area about as large as the United States, but if you put all of the land area together, you'd get about the size of Rhode Island, very small atolls but in a very large area.

In Ulithi we had an anchorage; it looked like a large ring. We had a net to cross where we'd go in, and we had our fleet in there [it could hold up to 700 ships] for this invasion of Okinawa. And I knew what was taking place right along, because I was on the radio.

The ships that were coming in there were unloading to the other ships right from the water. They couldn't even put it on land. There was just very little land for a staging area, you know? And one night, two suicide planes came in unannounced. I don't know if the Japanese fixed them in some nearby island, because we neutralized them all.[26] They hit this one carrier while they were watching movies. The other airplane came down and he saw an island lit up right

---

[26] March 11, 1945. Nearly two dozen planes had taken off from Japan, a distance of nearly 2,500 miles. At 10 p.m. at night, only two kamikazes arrived at the target area. The USS Randolph was the stricken carrier.

beside us; he thought it was a super dreadnought. He smashed into the island, and that was the end of him [*chuckles*].

Setting Sail for Okinawa

We then set sail for Okinawa in March of '45, which was over about 2,000 miles, patrolled by Japs. See, things happen quickly; we had the Japanese on the run, we were hitting them hard. The Philippines were still going on when we hit Okinawa—there were troops in Luzon, still in battle. As I remember it must have taken five or six days. We had such a force; I thought we'd go right to Japan! It was 60 miles long, protected with submarines and DEs like ours, for Japanese U-boats.

The Japanese spotted us, we knew it, and we could see that they were here. We pointed them out on radar, but they didn't dare attack. We shot a few planes down on the perimeter and knocked off a few subs. So I thought, boy we're going to take on Japan now, this will be the end. But when we got up there near Okinawa, it was on my birthday on March the 25th, there was a big bombardment. Okinawa was protected by the Japs for fifty years before we came! They had seven huge airfields there at that time. So we bombarded that that day and created quite a few fires; I think we hit oil tanks. Then we'd leave at night and come in early in the morning. One morning when we came in, they were taking off in the airstrips, and we gave them all the anti-aircraft fire we could. We got a few—not only our ships were firing, but so were many others.

We were the escort ship for the *Indianapolis*, you might have heard of it.[27] As a matter of fact, we would go in like a beagle dog,

---

[27] The USS *Indianapolis* was the heavy cruiser which would go on to deliver the parts for the first atomic bomb to the take-off base at Tinian Island. Sailing later for Leyte, she was torpedoed on July 30, 1945, sinking in less than 15 minutes with 300 men. The 900 other crew members spent the next five

close to the shore, and if a shell was fired, the *Indianapolis* fired a big one in. Our heaviest gun was only three-inch; that's about as heavy a shell as you can carry. It's nothing compared to what naval shells are. The *Indianapolis* had eight-inch. You couldn't handle an eight-inch shell yourself. So the *Indianapolis* was with us and we were with a sister ship, the *Bowers*, and two of the Japanese suicide planes aimed for the *Bowers* and us on the *Witter*; they were concentrating on our escort ships. One came for the *Bowers*, he came in a straight dive. Just before he hit, the *Bowers* made a quick turn, so just part of the wing hit it. And when the plane meant for us came, our ship did not fire quickly enough, and the *Indianapolis* did. Aboard the *Indianapolis* was Admiral Spruance, who was the Commander of the 5th Fleet. He gave our captain heck, so he got it for us that day, though we had gotten other suicide aircraft ourselves in the Philippines, under big attacks.

'We're Going to Be the Target'

On Easter Sunday, it would have been April the 1st of 1945 as I remember, the big invasion started, and on that day it wasn't too bad from what I would have expected, because troops and Marines were able to cut straight across the island. But now, pretty soon we found ourselves all alone. We were assigned to what was called 'roger [radar] picket duty.' We had to protect the island against the Japanese coming in to attack our troops; the attacks started getting worse and worse by kamikazes. One of my friends told me that battle was not so bad. He had only come onboard two months before, just coming from the States. I said, 'Yeah, that's true, until you're the target. We're going to be the target one of these days.'

---

days in a nightmare of battling sharks, exposure, and thirst and hunger. Only 317 survived the ordeal. [www.ussindianapolis.org/story.htm]

USS BUNKER HILL is hit off Okinawa by two kamikazes,
May 11, 1945. National Archives. Public domain.

On April the 6th we were under great attack all day. Our ship had to have oil [*refueling*], and we finally got it on. We had lunch about four o'clock, and right after that we had a big attack. Two of them came out of the skies and we fired like mad and got the first one. The other one was coming straight for us and we had him on fire. He hit into the engine room, fire room, and kitchen. He blew out about half of the ship with a thousand-pound bomb in the plane! Luckily he missed where I was, because on the other five ships in our group, most of the radiomen were dead, unless they were manning guns. You see, the kamikazes would aim for the bridge because it was the communication part of the ship, and they wanted to exterminate or get rid of all the destroyer escorts and destroyers so that they could come in and torpedo everything else. It was a good idea, but it didn't work out.

The kamikazes were coming from Japan. Okinawa might be just a few hundred miles from Japan, very close to Japan. So we were hit heavily and I saw quite a bit of action that day. One or two suicide planes went right through the noses of our ships, but several were shot down. When our ship was hit, I helped the gunners out all I could. One of our sister ships came up and towed us in to a little anchorage called Kerama Retto. Kerama Retto was not really controlled by us, except we used it for our ships. The Japanese planes would show up, and we'd fire at them. So we had the bait, and if we were under attack there, the Navy would use PT boats and make a big smoke ring, put in white smoke; you couldn't see anything, so they couldn't see us. But some of our ships would open up on the planes right through the smoke—our radar was so good that we'd shoot them right down. As a matter of fact, the radar on our ship was so efficient, we could spot a plane three hundred miles away! And we just traced them; if they came within 20 miles, we were all ready. That was a very good thing, we had good radar.

So we were in there from when we got hit at the beginning of April until June of 1945. There were so many ships that had been hit that we could not get a guy to weld it good enough to take us back to the United States. Finally, my lieutenant came up to me one day and he said we were going to take casualties back to the United States on the troop ship *USS Hocking*, a big ship, and that I could go with them because I had been there the longest. He said, 'When you get to California, you will take a leave, and then you will come back to California and our ship will be ready, and you will take it through the Panama Canal with the men who are [going to the East Coast].' So I went back on the *Hocking*; we were under great attack in a big convoy. We brought back a lot of amputees to Tinian to a big hospital there. Many of the men had legs off, arms off, maybe even all limbs off, a pitiful sight.

We got down there and we also put aboard the Seabees. We then went to the island of Kwajalein and then to Hawaii. We got off on a little base and they gave the destroyer escort men two beers every day. That's all I needed, I was drunk on two beers! I was 'landsick'; instead of being seasick, I was landsick. I was aboard a ship too long; I thought the land should hit me in the teeth! Then we came to San Francisco, and I had leave and came across the country, which I had to pay for, by the way. When I came back I found out the *Witter* had beaten me and had made it to California [*and then departed for the East Coast*], so they had to send me back again across the country!

Right about that time, World War II ended. And on September 28, 1945, I had enough points. I was in Philadelphia when the *Witter* came in, and I asked to get out. I got out and on October 1, I was in college! I wasted no time, one weekend.

'I Lost Many Friends'

Matthew Rozell: So what did you think about the atomic bomb?

Best thing that ever happened to us. If it wouldn't have been for the atomic bomb, I think we would have had a catastrophic amount of men killed, and probably the elimination of the Japanese nation as a whole. It would have been a terrible thing to conquer. I think it did a great deal in helping to save a million or two men, as well as the Japanese. I believe Harry Truman was a wonderful president in that regard; he really did a great favor to us. But I do not understand why we had to wait so long to figure things out! We shouldn't have gone into Okinawa if we knew we had the atomic bomb, because in Okinawa, we had 50,000 casualties! Our whole division was hit, except for the *Wilmarth*, as I told you. Two hundred and fifty ships were hit at Okinawa by kamikazes. The day we got hit, 26 ships got hit, and six were sunk to the bottom! I believe the Japanese had over 500 aircraft against us that day, suicide aircraft. Have you ever been startled by a partridge suddenly trying to fly into you? It is really a scary thing! They were nuts, like [angry] bees! Although you weren't thinking of it at the time, it was a scary thing that these people would give up their lives like that. It was the most Navy lives lost in one battle. I lost many friends.

*Destroyer Escort USS WITTER
following kamikaze attack. Alvin Peachman collection.*

As the land battle for Okinawa raged toward its crescendo with the fury of a storm, the kamikaze attacks would claim over 15,000 American casualties for the Navy alone.

CHAPTER FOURTEEN

Typhoon of Steel-Okinawa

After three years of fighting across 4,000 miles of ocean, the United States was finally poised at the threshold of the Japanese home islands. The island of Okinawa had been colonized by Japan in the early days of her imperial might; at a mere 340 miles from mainland Japan, the coming assault on the island would be an attack on her inner defenses. Sixty miles long and nearly 900 square miles, the island hosted perhaps 120,000 defenders, but once taken, planners reckoned it would be big enough to support 800 heavy bombers. As the winter of 1945 gave way to spring, it was clear to the Japanese that the island had to be held at all costs. Taking it was not going to be simple or easy. Planning for the largest combined operation in the Pacific War took months, and over half a million Americans would be committed to the battle.

Early morning on Easter Sunday, 1945, the invasion of Okinawa began. The first Marines and soldiers to hit the beaches that Easter morning were somewhat perplexed, however, to find little or no opposition. Others noted the irony of the date: besides being Easter Sunday, it was April 1- April Fools' Day.

Bruce Manell, a combat photographer from Whitehall with the 6th Marine Division, remembered the invasion.

Bruce Manell

They gave us a good time before we went to Okinawa. The Navy gave us all the beer we wanted to drink all day long. Oh, what a place that was [*Mog Mog, the island set aside for rest and relaxation at Ulithi*]!

When we hit the China Sea going into Okinawa—it is supposed to be one of the roughest seas in the world, and I won't deny that a bit—you would see ships go out of sight under the waves and coming back on top of the wave! The screws in the propellers came out of the water, and the whole ship vibrates because there is no water there, and you go back down. It was pretty rough. Anyway, we pulled up off Okinawa during the night, and about 1:00 in the morning, they woke us up to get ready to go ashore. I said I would go up topside to see what was going on. So I went up topside and—my golly!—guns were going off. That Navy, they really knew how to spit that stuff out! There were times when you could see the shape of a hill—with all the explosives going off at once. They were hitting a hill, and you could see the shape of the hill silhouetted in the dark. That was a tremendous barrage. Just about daybreak, they let off on that. And fighter planes and dive-bombers came in, and they did an awful job on the shore. That was a spectacular sight also. Then, at 20 minutes after 8:00, I went ashore with the first wave. You go to shore in one of these LCMs or LCVPs.[28] You have this big metal door in front of you, and they ram it into the shoreline. And as soon as it stops, the door flops down, and you wonder what's

---

[28] LCM was Landing Craft, Mechanized, capable of carrying one small tank or 100 troops. LCVP was the Landing Craft Vehicle/Personnel, also known as a Higgins boat; it could carry 36 troops or a small vehicle such as a Jeep.

going to be on the other side. There was nothing there! We were surprised. So we went ashore and started doing our job like we were supposed to, and guys were saying, 'Where's the Japs? Where are the Japs?' No one seemed to be able to find the Japs!

Then we started to get reports, a couple hours later— well, such-and-such has found some Japs south of us a ways. Then they started to get heavier and heavier resistance down there. So we found out where the war was...

Our job was to cut the island in two and then proceed north from there, which we did. We got scattered resistance here and there—except for one night, we had a banzai charge all over the island. They just seemed to come out of the ground, and it was 11:00 at night. It was a horrible night! I shot my first Jap then on Okinawa, and I have the grenade that he was trying to throw at me as a souvenir.[49]

'Mud and Total Extinction'

The Japanese were refining a defense–in–depth tactic that brought the battle up the island to the ten–mile–long Shuri Line. In the space of a very constricted area, some places no more than 600 yards wide, 300,000 fighting men were waging a death struggle that seemingly turned the area into a moonscape of exploding shells, knee–deep mud, denuded vegetation, sewage, and rotting corpses.[29]

---

[29] Author William Manchester, present at the fight, thought back to his father's experiences in World War I on the Western Front: *'This, I thought, was what Verdun and Passchendaele must have looked like. Two great armies, squatting opposite one another in mud and smoke, locked together in unimaginable agony . . . there was nothing green left...* 'See William Manchester, *Goodbye, Darkness: A Memoir of the Pacific War* (Boston: Little Brown, 1987) pp. 359–360.

Dan Lawler had recovered from his wounds at Peleliu and was back in the thick of things at Okinawa with his outfit, which included a friend of his from Alabama, Eugene B. Sledge. Sledge's war memoir would be published in the 1980s to vast critical acclaim.

*"Souvenirs". Dan Lawler (L) and Eugene Sledge (3rd from left) and others from 'K' Company on Okinawa.
Courtesy Dan Lawler.*

"Heavy rains began on May 6 and lasted through May 8, a preview of the nightmare of mud we would endure... until the end of the month. On May 8, Nazi Germany surrendered unconditionally...we were told the momentous news, but considering our own peril and misery...'so what' was typical of the remarks I heard around me. We were resigned to the fact that the Japanese would fight to total extinction on Okinawa, as they had elsewhere, and that Japan would have to be invaded with the same gruesome prospects. Nazi Germany might as well have been on the moon."[30]

---

[30] Sledge, Eugene B. *With the Old Breed at Peleliu and Okinawa*. New York: Oxford Univ. Press, 1981. 223. Mr. Lawler was well acquainted with the mild-mannered Alabamian Eugene Sledge (1923–2001), whom he would

Jim Butterfield recalled the island.

Jim Butterfield

Okinawa was a beautiful island, really. Gardens, a lot of farm-lands, and one of the problems we ran into there was civilians, which we never had before. You've got a lot to learn here, I think.

Our orders were that if we took anything—we were issued invasion money, and we were supposed to pay these people if we took a chicken. But some of those chickens we would put a .45 [cal. bullet] through, and we kept on going [*laughing*]. But it was pretty nice up there. It was hard with the people, because you did not know what... patrols would go out into the villages and stuff and get ambushed. The people that were living there, you'd think they were defending. So that is when we were ordered to take them out—put them in stockades. That wasted a lot of our time—slowed us up too.[50]

The Children in the Cave

It should also be noted that over 100,000 native Okinawan civilians were caught in the crossfire and killed.

Dan Lawler

We hit the middle of Okinawa. The Marines went north, and the Army went south. There were some civilians in a cave—we

tease as 'Rebel.' Unbeknownst to Lawler and his fellow infantrymen, Sledge was keeping notes of what was happening to them in his pocket–sized Bible. On publication of *With the Old Breed* in 1981, Mr. Sledge would be hailed as the most influential war memoirist of World War II. Ken Burns' PBS series, *The War* (2007) and the HBO series, *The Pacific* (2010) are based in part on his work. It is highly recommended for further reading.

couldn't get them out. So we talked to the interpreter. He said something in Japanese that meant 'Come out; we'll give you food and water.' So I went up to this cave and said that. No one came out, but I knew they were in there. They were talking very low. All of a sudden, a boy and girl came out... they came out of the mouth of the cave. And I could see that it was quite a ways away, so I stopped. They were about that tall [*gestures with hands, about three feet from ground*]. They finally came out a little bit closer. I moved a little bit closer. I got to where I could see they were shaking—they were shaken up. Their clothes were all blood—no socks, no shoes. And they were a mess—faces all blood—but they didn't have anyone around. So anyway, they would get just so far, and they wouldn't come any closer. I couldn't figure out what was the matter with them. And I figured, well, wait a minute, it might be the weapon. So I laid the weapon down, and I came back over.

And we had these candy bars... so I offered them that, but they wouldn't take it. I figured, well, maybe they figured there was something wrong. So I bit a piece off, and I gave the rest of it to him, and he bit a piece of that. Finally, he started talking to me in his own language, and grown-ups started coming out... so they all came out of the caves. And I picked the little girl up—she let me pick her up. It was rough—it was rough... [*pauses, then speaks in barely audible voice*] I still remember—I remember well... I can still see the two little kids... the Japanese told them that we were going to kill them, all those civilians: 'The Marines are going to kill all of you.'[51]

Evacuating the Wounded

Katherine Abbott was born in 1917 and wondered about her future upon graduation from South Glens Falls High School. Soon enough, she would find herself in the U.S. Army as a flight nurse during the Pacific War.

Katherine Abbott

I just wanted to do something. I wanted to be a school teacher, but we did not have enough money for me to go on to graduate school. We had a large family and we did not have that much money—we did not have student loans then. So someone suggested I would like nursing. I did apply and I went to Memorial Hospital in Albany for three years' service.

I think a friend of mine, a classmate, talked me into [the Army]. So we decided to go in, and after we heard about the Air Evacuation Squadron, and once we had our basic training, we applied for the School of Air Evacuation. It was six to eight weeks. Then we went overseas, this was 1944 and '45, and I was discharged in February 1946. My five brothers and I went into the service, and, as I said, my classmate talked me into going in, and, well, I thought it was a good idea.

In the Pacific, we shuttled from island to island, and [the wounded were] transferred from nurse to nurse, as you would in the wards when working shifts. Since there was only one nurse and one medical technician aboard the plane, we shuttled and changed planes and we rested until we were called again. So, we just kept things going—Hawaii, Johnson Island, Guadalcanal, Guam, Saipan, Tarawa, Biak, Leyte in the Philippines, and Okinawa; we would just be 'island hopping' with our planes. We had nothing to do with the Navy or the ships; they had their own Navy nurses and Navy nurse corps. We flew day and night, so where we were all depended on how the war was going and [where we were needed in] getting the patients ready to be transferred.

We were on call as the patients were being transferred and brought in by ambulance. We would be there to see that they were put on the plane and to secure their litters to the walls of the plane. They had hooks with a certain snap to them to make sure they were safe. The [aircraft] were four-motored cargo planes. On cargo planes, all the way back, there was nothing but space, and that is where we put the patients, on each side of the walls of the plane and down the center, and it was just the nurse and the technician, the medical technician. There was no doctor.

We had 28 patients on the plane. We carried three tiers of four patients on each tier on each side, and four patients on the center of the plane on the floor. We had some patients who were ambulatory and others that couldn't move, but they were on the top layers. We did not have anyone who was really, really bad, because our planes were not pressurized and [had] no oxygen, so we could not go any higher than 9,000 or 10,000 feet. That is what you call 'primitive,' because we were the pioneers in air evacuation and they had just started. Today I believe they are much improved, and they have the helicopters.

Mostly we were looking after them and administering pain medication. We had one tuberculosis patient, bleeding, coughing up blood, and he was the only one we had sitting up on the one seat we had there. Usually, most of it was pain; codeine and morphine were the only medications we carried, and then we had penicillin. We gave penicillin shots every three hours. We had no 'facilities,' you might say, for any medical treatments or anything aboard plane; this was mostly for transport and keeping them comfortable. As I said, that was ancient. We were just starting out and it was the best we could do. I believe today they must have everything more so than we did. Of course that was quite a while ago, but you know, we did the job.

The patients were on the plane continuously until they got to Hawaii, then I do not know what they did. They probably rested, and once they had been checked out, they would take the long trip home. This was definitely discharge; they would not be going back into battle. We also had prisoners of war. Once I had a plane full of prisoners of war, 28, they were all ambulatory and walking around; I remember that one plane full.

They tried to have the safest planes for us. Sometimes something was wrong with the plane and we had to go back and change all of the patients and had them all moved into the new plane, but that didn't bother me. I was not scared of enemy fliers, because they had fighter pilots on call or on the alert all the time.

We were not at the battle areas at all except for the trips to Okinawa. We went in at midnight and we flew in from Guam or Saipan or Tinian for eight hours. We took off at midnight, so we landed at 8 o'clock in the morning, daylight, and on the first trip I had, our Navy was shelling the southern tip of Okinawa and that is the closest I ever came [to the battle zone]. The Japs did fly below the radar on the island at Biak as I was stationed there. I had taken off with a load of patients at 7:00 p.m. and they flew in at 7:30 p.m. while we were loading another plane! They just dropped the one bomb, but no one was really injured. They hit the area, but that is the only time I came close to any actual fighting. But we had to make it pretty safe for the patients, you know at the time, as we were transporting them.

Nurses relaxing, Guam. Donald P.Quarters collection.
Courtesy Jackie Quarters.

'You've got nothing to work with, Jimmy.'

Within the space of seven weeks, the band of 1ˢᵗ Marine Division broth-ers from the North Country near the "Falls"—who had forged their bonds at boot camp and in combat at Peleliu—would be broken up for good. Jack Murray of Hudson Falls was stateside with his knee wound sustained on Peleliu; Harold Chapman of Gansevoort and Jim Butterfield of Glens Falls would be the next to fall.

Jim Butterfield

On Okinawa, you have to remember, we were only about 150 miles from Japan itself. Japan was next on the list after Okinawa. So every day and every night you would get air raids. They had young kids flying these planes—they were dying for the Emperor. It was a great thing to do. You were going to go up there to heaven, or so they said.

When you looked back on Buckner Bay at night, you would see all our ships would go back out to sea—because it was dangerous to stay around. We had two hospital ships there. The hospital ships would be lit up at night, and the Red Cross was supposed to be on them. These guys [*the Japanese*] weren't supposed to hit the hospital ships. But I was up on the ridge, and I said to my friend Chappy, 'If I get hit, Chappy, you make sure they don't put me aboard one of those things.' But Chappy got it before that.

Harold Chapman and Jimmy had been through boot camp together, and were in the same outfit, G Company, 2nd Battalion, 1st Marines, where Jimmy was the squad leader. Jim usually checked in with his friend every morning, but on May 5, Jim was tending to one of his badly wounded men and did not see him. Word came to him later in the day that Harold was killed.[31] The loss affected him deeply. Sixty years later, he recalled, 'It really took the wind out of my sails.' Not even the letters from his steady girlfriend back home, Mary, cheered him much in the weeks to follow.[32]

Still on the Shuri Line, Jim was severely wounded in the head two weeks later. Over 60 years afterward he came to my classroom with his

---

[31] Harold Chapman's remains were repatriated nearly four years after he was killed on Okinawa. He joined the Marine Corps in 1943 at the age of 17. He was survived by three sisters and his mother, whom Jimmy Butterfield and Danny Lawler visited upon their return home in 1945. 'Body of U.S. Marine Being Returned Home', *The Glens Falls Post-Star,* March 7, 1949.

wife Mary and good friend Dan Lawler. His humor still intact and on display, Jim poignantly recalled the experience of struggling to accept the fact that he would never see again.

Jim Butterfield

I enlisted into the United States Marine Corps the seventh of December, 1943. I was seventeen years old then and I went because I wanted to help fight the good war. My mother didn't want me to go. Mary didn't want me to go. But I heard they threw a party after I left. [*Laughter*]

Mary Butterfield:

Yes, we went to school together and Jimmy left six months before graduation. I told him, 'Don't go until after you graduate,' but he wanted to go. He was afraid the war would be over before he could get in. So he went in, in December, and I graduated in June.

Matthew Rozell: You were high school sweethearts?

Jim Butterfield:

Mary and I have been palling around for over 60 years now.

Mary Butterfield:

Well, we've been married 61 years.

Jim Butterfield:

She couldn't wait to get married, but I think she's changed her mind a couple times since then... [*Laughter*]

It was an exciting time, it was an adventurous time, and it was a proud time. I lasted 61 or 62 days up to Okinawa before I got hit. Danny was fortunate—he got all the way through. Right, Dan?

Dan Lawler: Ninety-eight days I was there.

Matthew Rozell: Mary, do you remember getting the news that Jim was wounded?

Mary Butterfield:

Yes, I remember. This girl who lived on our street was going steady with this Navy corpsman, and he wrote a letter to her, telling her that Jimmy was very bad, that he was wounded through the eye. She came over that Saturday morning, I remember, and she told me. I was surprised, and I called his mother. And she said that she got a letter from the government only telling her that he was wounded. But that's the way that I found out about it, about how he was wounded on Okinawa.

Jim Butterfield:

Well, the first letter that they got was telling them that I was temporarily blind at the time. When I got hit, we were going to take Shuri Castle, because the 6th Division was already in there, and they were catching it real bad. So they decided to put us in there to pull some of the people away from them—to give them a hand.

We were doing very well. It was a beautiful day when we started out. I had gotten seven Japs when they attacked the perimeter that night, and I thought I had a good day in front of me. So as we were moving along, somebody behind me yelled, 'Whitey just got it!' He was a friend of ours.[32] So I turned around, and I saw him rolling down the ridge. He got it in the head, and the face too. So I told this Marine next to me to take the squad, I'll be right back. I figured it was an easy job to do because it was downhill. So I ran down and grabbed Whitey by his belt. We went over a little ridge, and I thought we had enough shelter.

---

[32] Marine Corporal 'Whitey' Hargus.

Wana Ridge. Shuri Line. "A Marine of the 1st Marine Division draws a bead on a Japanese sniper." National Archives. Public domain.

Then a couple of other guys came. I said, 'Look it, we have to get a corpsman up here, I think Whitey's going to go into shock.' You see when you got hit, you didn't always die from the wound. Sometimes you went into shock. Shock could kill you. So I turned around to say something to him, and that's the last I remember. I don't know where that guy, the shot, came from. I got it with a rifle [shot].

I lost part of the right side of my face. I don't know if it was a day, or two days later—I don't even know really what happened to me—the enemy laid a mortar barrage when I was on my way to the hospital at the beach, and I got hit again, in the face! That took care of the other side of my face. I was 14 months in the hospital having my face rebuilt, and that's why I am so good-looking today. [*Laughter*]

This is a small world we live in. A guy named Joe Gavita from Glens Falls was the corpsman at that station. Of course I knew Joe before that, and Joe was taking care of me! I don't remember this at all. He said I carried on a conversation with him. I was telling him how bad it was up there. I don't remember that. The next thing I remember is I woke up in that station and what a headache I had! Oh! Talk about a hangover!

The corpsman came and said, 'How are you doing?' I said, 'How about loosening up these bandages, they're killing me.' He said, 'No can do.' So I sat up in the sack and started to unroll it myself. The next thing I know, I got a shot in the arm and I was knocked out again. The next time I woke up, I woke up in an aircraft. A C-54 transport. I never flew before. I had no idea where the hell I was! I put my hand out on the deck, and I just could not put it together—that I was in a plane! Someone must have had a word out to keep an eye on me, because the next time I reached out there, there was a patent leather shoe. I moved my hand a little bit, and there was a nice ankle with a silk stocking! [*Some laughter*] I thought, 'Jesus, I have died and have gone to heaven!' [*Much laughter from students*] I started running my hand up that leg, and she said, 'I think you've gone far enough.' [*More laughter*]

She said to me, 'Jimmy, would you like a turkey sandwich and a glass of milk?' I said, 'Real milk?' She said, 'Real milk.' I said, 'You bet your life!' She brought it down, and there had to be something in it, because I was out again. I woke up in Guam, in the hospital. I was there about three weeks, I guess. I got an operation there. I didn't know they did it. But what was left of my left side of the eye and face, they took out. Now see, these people knew that I was not going to see again.

The doctor came up. I said, 'How am I doing, Doc? I have to go back up there. They're short of people.' He said, 'You're doing fine, my young boy.' That was all I would get, see? Do you want to hear this whole story? [*Teenagers: Yes!*]

They took me to Honolulu. The nurse said, 'You're going to like it.' I said, 'Yeah, that will be nice. Now how about a cigarette?' [*To the young people*] We smoked them then; we didn't know they killed you... So she said, 'No, you can't. They're putting fuel in the plane.' I said, 'I'm dying for one—let me have one.' Then she let me have one.

We flew into Hawaii, and it was a beautiful hospital. It was overlooking the Pacific. Down below you could see Diamond Head. Now, I couldn't see any of these things. But I was told all of this stuff.

I still had the bandages on. They were teaching you little things, like to sit down at the tray, how to eat. Now, the first thing they teach you is, you work by the clock—like your milk would be at 1:00, your bread at 9:00, your potatoes at 6:00. Things like that you had to start learning, see... I went along with this, still not thinking— and this is how stupid that you can be—that I wasn't going to see again. Nothing in my mind thought that [being blind] was going to happen to me. I was getting around. I always had somebody with me.

So this one day, we were sitting there, and this guy said, 'Jimmy, I bet you five bucks you can't go to the head and back in five minutes.' Five dollars is pretty good money. I had done it before already, so I said, 'Yeah, I'll bet you.' So I did a good job—I got to the men's room, the head. But when I came back, I took a quarter of a step wrong, and I ended up in a long, not-too-wide closet, and I didn't know how the hell to get out of there! Then I start sweating. I was all bandaged up, and underneath my bandages was Vaseline, gauze. I thought, 'Geez, I've got to get out of here!' Five bucks is five bucks, and I had lost it already.

I finally got out of there, and I went over and sat down. I said, 'How about a cigarette?' Someone handed me a cigarette. There was a Zippo lighter. Guy goes like this [*holds hand up, makes flicking motion with thumb*]. My whole face goes up in flames! [*Laughter*] I had this guy who was nearsighted next to me, trying to put it out [*he laughs*], and all he did was fan the flames... you'd think you were back in the foxhole again! The nurse comes running over, and off go the bandages. Fortunately, I did not get burned. So she says, 'Give me your lighter! Give me your cigarettes!' She took them away from me. So all day long, I'm bumming cigarettes and a lighter. Then I'm going over and putting them underneath my mattress. Now that nurse is standing there watching me do this, and I don't know she's doing this. So I get up about 4:00—I feel under the mattress. There was no lighter, no cigarettes. The nurse says, 'You want a cigarette, Jimmy?' [*Laughter*]

I'm sitting there one day with one of the guys that was just in from Okinawa. I was asking how they were doing and stuff, and this guy sticks his head in the door. He says, 'I'm looking for Jim Butterfield.' I said, 'He's right here, what do you want?' He says, 'It's Dick Barber, Jim.' Now this is Dr. Barber from Glens Falls.[33] I had no idea how he knew I was there. He was stationed there. I get a nice lieutenant-colonel walking into my room—my stock automatically goes up! He says, 'Let me look at your face.' I said, 'Dick, you can't do that. This is a Navy hospital, I think they'll frown on an Army guy doing this.' He said, 'I want to see what they're doing to you.' So he looked. This man knew right there that I was never going to see again. He never said a word to me. I don't think he ever told anybody back here at home.

---

[33] Well-known Glens Falls doctor Charles Richard Barber (1914–1999).

I didn't know, until they told me there.

So here's the climax. Every morning there was inspection with the doctors. So the doctor came around that morning. He said, 'How are you, Jim?' I said, 'Fine.' He said, 'You need anything?' I said, 'Nope, I'm doing fine.' He says, 'Well, are you used to the idea?' I said, 'Used to what idea?' He said, 'That you're not going to see again.'

Well, you could hear a pin drop. I said, 'I don't think I heard you, Doc.' He said, 'You're not going to see again.' I said, 'What?' He said, 'Didn't they tell you in Guam?'

I said, 'No! But it's a good thing that [first] doctor isn't here, because I'd kill him!' I got so mad! I couldn't really grab the idea. I'm not going to see again? ... What the hell did I know about blindness? Nothing!

I said, 'How about operations?' He said, 'You've got nothing to work with, Jimmy.'

So a pat on the shoulder, and he just walks away. The nurse comes over and says, 'The doctor wants you to take this pill.' I said, 'You know what the doctor can do with that pill?'

Mary Butterfield:
Don't say it.

Jim Butterfield:
I'm not going to, Mary.

So I had a hard... two months, I guess. I kept mostly to myself. I wouldn't talk to people. I tried to figure out what the hell I was going to do when I got home. How was I going to tell my mother this? You know what I mean?

So they come around and said, 'You've got a phone call.' So I went in to where the phone was. They were calling me from home. They got the message, see... This one here was on the phone [*points to Mary*]. I said, 'Looks like things have changed, kiddo.' She said,

'No, we'll discuss this when you get home.' She was already bossing me around. [*Laughter*]

But that's how I found out, and that's how it happened. And after a while, I just started to live with it.

There are not days—even today—I go to bed and I wish I could see. So much I miss. I miss watching a nice girl walking down the street. I miss seeing my daughter, my wife. I even miss looking at Danny. [*Laughter*]

Mary Butterfield:

But you see, I'm only 17 to you now. That's a good thing.

Jim Butterfield:

Since we got in the conversation, when I dream, and I do dream, everything is real. Everything I knew before, I see it as it was then, not today. My wife and daughter would never get old in my eyes. When I dream of Mary, she's still seventeen years old.

Mary Butterfield:

But you never saw your daughter.

Jim Butterfield:

I dream about my daughter. Mary's caught me doing this. We lost our daughter a year and a half ago. But I sit right up in bed and I'm trying to push away that little cloud of fog in front of her, but I can't quite make her out.

Mary says, 'What are you doing?' I say, 'Just dreaming.'

Jim Butterfield was nineteen years old at the Battle of Okinawa. [53]

In the final push at the Shuri Line that cost him his eyesight, the Marines lost over 3,000 men and the U. S. Army even more. When the island was declared secure near the end of June, in Lawler's K/3/5, only 26 Peleliu veterans who had landed with the company had survived Okinawa. It had been the bloodiest campaign of the Pacific, with over 12,500 Americans killed or missing and nearly three times that number wounded. For the Japanese, no accurate counts are possible, but perhaps 110,000 were killed. [54]

Jim Butterfield, 2000.
Author photo.

CHAPTER FIFTEEN

Redemption

As spring 1945 turned to summer, Okinawa had fallen, the war in Europe had ended, and the air raids over Japan were reaching a crescendo. In Japan, the prisoners tried to hang on. For many men, punishment was becoming more severe, and resignation and despair set in to overwhelm them. Joseph Minder was still slaving in the copper mine in northern Japan, but was determined to remain focused on survival, and getting home.

Unbroken

Joe Minder

July to early August, 1945

Johnson and Milchesky started working at the shop. I started working at the bottom of the mine. Very dangerous down there, because of many cave-ins and rocks rolling down from the four levels above, however the work there is much easier than pushing and loading dirt carts, so I'll take my chances.

More air raids every day now. Getting soya beans in small amounts. We got so weak last month and so darn many men passed out on the job that the Japs realized they wouldn't be able to get any more work out of us unless our diet was picked up a bit. No one has gained any weight, but at least we aren't passing out on the job anymore.

'A Question Until The End of Time'

Well before the fighting on Okinawa was over, planning was complete for the invasion of Japan. The invasion, code named 'Downfall,' was to be in two stages. The first, Operation Olympic, would take place on the southern island of Kyushu on November 1. Phase two, Operation Coronet, would use Kyushu as a staging area for the invasion of the Tokyo plain in March 1946.[55]

In this narrative, we must suspend for the moment arguments about the moral legitimacy of the bomb, and focus on the facts of the day and the voices of the veterans themselves. When President Truman and the Allies demanded Japan's unconditional surrender after the successful July testing of the atomic bomb in the sands of New Mexico, the reality was that up to one-third of the American invasion force in the battle for Okinawa was killed, wounded, or missing. Invasion planners were certain that the coming invasion figures would be grimmer. It is also true that the Japanese prison camp commandants, since 1943, had been given the "kill-all" order in the event of imminent invasion, a policy which was carried out on numerous occasions and updated, reinforced, and clarified as time went on.[56]

From the Potsdam Conference in defeated Germany, President Truman warned the Japanese to surrender. On August 6, 1945, a single bomb tumbled from a B–29 Superfortress flying from Tinian in the Mariana Islands. Hiroshima was devastated by both the blast and thermal and radioactive effects that would lead later estimators to put the death toll at 140,000.

John W. Norton, a seaman on the repair ship USS Vulcan, was there shortly afterwards.

John Norton

We were in Hiroshima at the time they signed the official surrender. I was there almost six months, anchored off Hiroshima, and I spent a lot of time in the city. When we got there it was just leveled, and there were two shells of buildings—one was a hospital and one was a school—and those were the only buildings that looked like they had been buildings. We walked around. The people, the civilians, were looking at us wondering what we were going to do to them. And, oh my God, the scars on their faces and burns. Oh God, it was sickening. Women and children—it was just sickening.

Asked if he thought the bomb was necessary, Mr. Norton replied, 'Well, that has been the question, and it will be the question until the end of time, I guess, but it saved many lives.'

Ralph Leinoff was resting up from combat at Iwo Jima and preparing for the inevitable.

Ralph Leinoff

I was tired and I was disgusted. I knew that I still had another landing to make, and while out in the field at Maui doing the training exercises for Japan, we got word that something happened, that a bomb wiped out an entire city of people and that the bomb may end the war.

I couldn't believe it. We had been fighting the Japanese for three years and I felt no one bomb is going to make them turn around and change their mind; they're going to fight to the death. Everyone in the Japanese Army was told, 'You're going to die, but you have to take ten Marines with you; before you die, you take ten Marines with you!' So when the word came about Hiroshima, suddenly it seemed like maybe there was a chance we would not have to do that landing.

We had a new company captain at that time—he called us together. He said, 'Look, fellas, this is just a rumor, we can't go by it. We know how tough the enemy is, we're going to put all our heart and soul into these training exercises, because as far as we know, we're going to have to land on Japan. It's going to be a brutal, brutal thing. Japan is going to be really bad.' Three days later word of Nagasaki came and he called us together again. He said, 'Well, there is a possibility we may not have to do it, but just for old times' sake, go through the exercises you're supposed to do.' [*laughs*]. So we went through training exercises, but I never got to Japan.

With no answer to the call for surrender coming from the Japanese High Command, on August 9 the second (and last) bomb was deployed against Nagasaki in southeastern Japan. The death toll was at least 70,000. Marine Walter Hooke had occupation duty in Nagasaki.

Walter Hooke

We landed in Sasebo [the major naval base in Nagasaki Prefecture]. Every city in our first few months there, we went from one end... to the other, and every city was flattened, you know. I have some pictures I can show you. There is nothing in the cities—they were wiped out, they were worse than Nagasaki—but Sasebo, the town we landed in, appeared more devastated compared to Nagasaki—except I saw the difference.

When I got to Nagasaki, there were all these people around that had been burned and injured, and the hospitals were overflowing. They could not take care of people, and you know, I did not get there in Nagasaki until October—and from the bomb [I could see] there had been people with skin hanging off. It was awful.

Roman Catholic cathedral on a hill in Nagasaki.
National Archives. Public domain.

On the radio the Japanese Emperor Hirohito spoke to his people and said, 'The time has come when we must bear the unbearable.' It was the first time they had heard his voice. Shaken prison camp commandants awaited word of whether or not to carry out the "kill-all" order within their camps.

Joe Minder recorded his observations as the prisoners dared to hope that their redemption was near.

Joe Minder

August 15, 1945

Heavy bombing near here all last night. Terrific explosions. *12:00 a.m.:* All Japs went to town. We didn't go to work until 3 p.m.—something is darn funny around here. Guards are very quiet today.

August 16, 1945

Many peace rumors floating around camp today.

August 17, 1945

Australian officers received paper written in Japanese. They say the war is over from what they could interpret in the paper.

August 18, 1945

Worked in garden near camp a half day. Heard loudspeakers blaring away downtown.

August 19, 1945

Camp commander announced we would not work in the mine anymore. War must be over?

August 20, 1945

War's end was officially announced by interpreter, 'Mosiki,' at 1:15 p.m.! Still hard to believe![34]

---

[34] Lester Tenney, a Bataan Death March survivor and fellow slave laborer at a mine in Japan, recalled testing the guards to get a feel for whether or not the war was really over. He left his barracks and offered a "Hello" in Japanese to the nearest guard he could find, a move that normally would have resulted in a severe beating, as he deliberately did not bow. Instead, the

August 21, 1945

Four prisoners who escaped from camp June 18 returned and were turned loose with us. They told us of the horrible brutal treatment they received after being captured by Japs.

Now, the moment of liberation was at hand. It would stay in the ex-prisoners' minds for the rest of their lives.

August 22, 1945

After three and a half years of starvation and brutal treatment, that beautiful symbol of freedom once more flies over our head! Our camp tailor worked all night and finished our first American flag! The blue came from a GI barracks bag, red from a Jap comforter, and the white from an Australian bed sheet. When I came out of the barracks and saw those beautiful colors for the first time, I felt like crying!

I know now, like I never did before, what it means to be able to live in a peaceful nation like the U.S.A. with its unlimited amount of liberties and freedom.

Japs increased our chow. An 800-pound bull was brought in camp. Had fried fish and fried greens and fried tomatoes, also a level bowl of barley/soya bean/thick blood soup for supper.

August 25, 1945

Twelve American planes flew over near camp! Large *"PW"* signs were nailed onto the roofs, and also a huge sign made out of blackout shades and white paper by the Australian officers saying

---

guard returned the salutation in English, with deference. In a 2014 interview, Tenney recalled with emotion, "He bowed to me. He bowed, to *me!*"

"*SMOKES—CANDY—NEWS—300*" was placed on the ground in front of our barracks, in the hopes that the Yanks would spot our signs and drop us supplies!

6:00 p.m.

Capt. Beadstine just announced that our parents had been notified of our whereabouts.

Bundles from Heaven

August 28, 1945

What an exciting day!

This morning we were waiting anxiously for the two cigarettes which the Japs issue each day, as their daily issue, and wondering if we would receive a level bowl of barley and beans for dinner. Our food, clothing, and cigarette worries finally ended at 4 o'clock this afternoon. About 2:00 p.m., two American planes zoomed real low over our camp, then circled around again and dropped a note saying, "*OK boys, read your message. Stand clear, supplies will be dropped shortly.*" About 20 minutes later they returned escorting Grumman dive bombers and a B–29 and started dropping tons of candy, smokes, food, clothing, and medicine, with large parachutes. I don't think I have seen a more beautiful and exciting sight in my life! We could watch the men in the rear of the plane tumble those huge bundles of blessings out, then huge cargo parachutes of all different colors opened, and the food which we have been waiting for three and a half years started falling like rain all over our campground!

This continued until 4:00 p.m., when the B–29 opened and closed its bomb bay doors, signaling us, 'that is all,' and flew away. Men started running around, excited as heck, gathering up the large bundles scattered inside and outside the compound on the roofs and downtown, where one heavy load was dropped by a B–29 in a muddy rice paddy, burying many large drums deep in the mud when they broke loose from their parachutes. Several large bundles also broke loose from the parachutes over our camp and riddled many barracks full of large holes as if bombs had been dropped on us.

Bill Fisher and an Australian officer were killed by falling bundles. Bill was killed instantly when two large 55–gallon drums broke loose from the parachutes and crashed through the side of the barracks about eight feet from where my bed was located![57]

5:00 p.m.

Left camp to help dig supplies out of rice paddies and haul them back to camp. Much food was broken open, so I filled my gut with candy, canned fruit, army ration, and God-knows-what-not. I'll never forget the first taste of American food I had! I salvaged a small amount of cocoa, a cube of pineapple, and Type-C crackers on the road on my way downtown.

8:00 p.m.

It started raining hard, so I returned back to camp, barefoot, wet, muddy, and cold, but with a full gut and as happy and excited as a kid would be just after Santa Claus left!

August 29, 1945:

About 10:00 a.m., a B–29 dropped a large load of supplies outside of camp. I helped haul it back to camp. Got several candy bars from boxes of candy which Mayhue and Johnson carried in.

August 31, 1945:

Very sick this morning and last night from overeating. Just don't know when to stop; this food tastes so darn delicious!

11:00 a.m.

Truck just brought in another big load of supplies dropped by mistake by a B–29 at a Japanese camp about 80 miles from here!

The View from Tokyo Bay

On September 2, 1945, Admiral "Bull" Halsey's flagship USS Missouri was in Tokyo Bay awaiting the arrival of the Japanese delegation with General MacArthur and Admiral Nimitz aboard, positioned in the exact spot where Commodore Matthew C. Perry had anchored on his first visit to Japan in 1853, and flying his original 31-star flag.[58] The Japanese delegation was escorted promptly aboard at 9:00 a.m. and signed the terms of surrender. In the United States and Europe, it was six years to the day that the bloodiest conflict in human history had begun. Joseph Marcino, a Marine tank commander on Iwo Jima from the North Country, was on board one of the many ships in the bay as a witness to history.

Joe Marcino

What a sight that was! When daylight came, you could not see a place on the ocean where there was not a ship. The bay was just filled with all ships—massive, a lot more than Iwo Jima. At that time, we had some inkling we were going to make a landing on Japan. And so we were in that position, with ships as far as you could see on the horizon. The ocean was just full of destroyers, battleships, cruisers, and landing craft—just everything.

Surrender ceremonies, 2,000 plane flyover, USS MISSOURI left foreground.
National Archives. Public domain.

The Redeemed Captive

As the Japanese delegation signed the instrument of surrender, General MacArthur concluded the ceremony: 'It is my earnest hope, indeed the hope of all mankind, that from this solemn occasion a better world shall emerge from the blood and carnage of the past.' Present just behind him on the deck for the honor of the occasion was the newly liberated General Jonathan Wainwright, who had spent much of his captivity leading his men (including John Parsons, who was imprisoned with him on Formosa) in defying the Japanese. Once the signatures were all in order, the 11-man Japanese delegation was immediately escorted off the ship. The awesome task of reconstructing and restoring civilization could begin, but for most of the prisoners of war, the journey towards home and healing had not even gotten underway.

Joe Minder

September 1, 1945

Feeling good again, going to try and take it a little easy on that rich food. Had pictures taken and got weighed this afternoon. Gained four and a half pounds in seven days.

September 3, 1945

Many men sick from overeating. Camp baking oven completed today. Had 20 doughnuts for supper, first since May 1942. Had baggage inspection this morning. We are getting packed ready to leave!

6:00 p.m.

Had chocolate-covered cupcakes for supper—they were delicious!

September 4, 1945

B–29s dropped supplies at Camp 6 and 8 today. Still waiting for our food drop. Had biscuits for supper. First type of bread since April 1942. They were made out of Jap barley flour.

September 5, 1945

Fifteen large sacks of potatoes and a dressed horse came in this afternoon. A B–29 circled over camp several times but didn't drop anything.

7:00 p.m.

Just finished hearing my first American voice over the radio since the fall of Corregidor in May 1942. [The commander was] urging us to remain in our camps and we would be evacuated from Japan as soon as possible.

September 6, 1945

Heard our first American news broadcast at noon: 4,000 POWs have already been liberated, 14% of the total POWs here in Japan.

September 9, 1945

Killed fat horse this morning. Had delicious horse steak and horse blood gravy for supper, also few Irish spuds and rice.

September 11, 1945

Stayed up until 12:30 last night with Bradley eating and drinking coffee. Got weighed, gained 13 pounds in the past 19 days!

3:00 p.m.

Waiting here in the camp yard, packed, ready to march to the train to meet the Yanks at the sea coast. God, what a crazy-looking bunch we are! Baggage of all sorts strapped to our backs. Some are packs made of different colored parachutes, blankets, Red Cross boxes, and some even have their belongings in old packed barracks bags which originally came from Bataan or Corregidor. Our pockets and shirts are crammed full of candy, gum, cigarettes, canned food, God-knows-what-all. Wish I had a picture of the entire bunch!

6:00 p.m.

Just got on train for our 13–hour train ride to the coast!

Like scores of others like it, the ex-POW train clacked and snaked through the Japanese countryside, slowing to pass through firebombed cities, which were now just charred husks of their former glory, peopled in some places only with the silent, dazed, and desperate. At the port of Yokohama, the soldiers disembarked and began the second leg of their long journey home.

Joe made it back to the Philippines, where he found he had been promoted to corporal. He was booked on a troop transport with 3,200 other Americans and headed for home.

October 10, 1945

We are sailing past Corregidor, Fort Hughes, Fort Drum, and the Bataan peninsula now. Although we are quite a distance from these fortified islands, we can still see the result of the terrible bombings and shellings which these forts took from both the Japs and Americans. I can see Monkey Point on Corregidor very plainly from this side of the ship now. That is where the Japs finally forced us to surrender after battering away at us with bombs and shells for five months.

6:30 p.m.

In a few minutes now we will be able to get the last glimpse of the battlefields where our buddies lie, unfortunate not to be going home with us. Never thought when I sailed into this bay on October 23, 1941, that these small green tropical islands would be hot battlefields within two months.

Three weeks later, Joe arrived in San Francisco.

November 1, 1945

Up ready for breakfast, couldn't sleep very much last night. Thinking of landing kept me awake!

8:30 a.m.

There she is! Off in the distance we can see a faint glimpse of the Golden Gate lying in a dense bank of fog. A beautiful day! In a few minutes the beautiful, tall buildings in San Francisco will be visible!

8:45 a.m.

Shouts and cheers rang out all over the entire ship as 3,200 men and army nurses clung to every possible point from deck to top mast, watching the boat pass under the Golden Gate! Boy, what a wonderful feeling!

11 a.m.

Tied up at Pier 15 now. Mothers, sisters, and friends are going wild down on the pier as they spot men that they know, who are clinging to the rails, life boats, and what-not. Boy, there are some swell-looking girls down there! Those Yank gals are as good-looking as ever!

12:15 p.m.

Officers have started down the gang plank. Major Warmuth's sister and mother are kissing him and going crazy with joy! There are also a large bunch of newspaper reporters around, trying to get a story from him.

1:00 p.m.

Arrived at Letterman Hospital by bus from pier! It's a great feeling riding up a modern city street again!

Thanksgiving, 1945, would find Joe at home in North Creek, New York, with his family for the first time in nearly four years. The joyful reunion was tempered with his learning of the passing of his mother while he was in captivity, but after months in and out of hospitals he would find solace in the quiet of the mountains, streams, and lakes of the Adirondacks. He found skiing, which he had taken up at the age of seven, to be particularly therapeutic as he slowly gained back some of his strength. During his visits to his doctor, he noticed a young lady who worked in the office, and began to offer her a ride home after his appointments. In 1948, Joe Minder and Hazel Allen were married and settled down to raise two boys. He worked out of the office of the local garnet mine and also in the fledgling ski industry that began to take off after World War II. He gave back to his community with a commitment to his church, fire department, and other civic organizations, and patiently taught the youth how to ski and even how to properly cultivate a garden. Despite the physical effects of those Japanese clubs or the 16-hour days carrying 70 pound bags of Japanese copper ore, which took their toll on his body as time progressed, Joe never harbored any bitterness or hatred for the horrible suffering he had experienced as a young man. He did not talk often about his prisoner experience, but his ethos of patience, kindness, and compassion for others shines forth in his journal and was confirmed in the way he lived out his days. The entire community grieved when Joseph Minder passed away in 2006 at age 88; the little town's ski bowl lodge would be named after him.

*

'Lost is the Youth We Knew'

A poem composed by Lt. Henry G. Lee, a Bataan survivor and fellow prisoner, was discovered during the daring American rescue raid on Cabanatuan Camp at the end of January 1945. Perhaps Lee's feelings, written so near to the end and hidden in the journal of poems he was forced to leave behind, sum up the conflicting emotions of so many of the young defenders of the Philippines, and all the men who fought in the Pacific.

Westward we came across the smiling waves,
West to the outpost of our country's might
'Romantic land of brilliant tropic light'
Our land of broken memories and graves.

Eastward we go and home, so few
Wrapped in their beds of clay our comrades sleep
The memories of this land are branded deep
And lost is the youth we knew.[59]

Lt. Henry G. Lee never got to go home; he had been killed in one of the American air raids on the unmarked hellships in Takao Harbor in Formosa, just three days before Joe Minder began his own voyage from there to his final destination at the mine in Japan.

World War II had formally ended, but back in "Hometown, USA," the returning survivors, their families, and the families of those who did not return would see the legacy of the war last far beyond the end of 1945.

John Norton

There was a family that lost two sons in World War II. The family got a telegram on a Monday that one of the boys was killed, and that Thursday they got another telegram saying that his brother had been killed. There were about 35 young men from Granville who were killed in World War II, and I knew every one of them. Some of them were older, and some of them were younger; most of them were good friends of mine.[35]

Ralph Leinoff

I was one of the lucky ones who managed to escape essentially unharmed physically; but there is no doubt that when you see men die around you and when you're holding dying men in your arms, it has an effect on you. Even when things calm down you start to think about it, you see things that happen when a man is begging to see his wife and children one more time before he dies, you can't help it. I mean, that has an effect on you.

When I was able to come home, I married the girl I knew from infancy. We had a good life and I got a job, we had children, but I slept for the first two years of marriage and children with a Bowie knife beside my bed, because I could still see Japanese coming at me in the dark. It was just something that I felt secure about; I had to have a knife beside me, but I got away from that.

Physically I was in good shape, but psychologically, there is some trauma. If you're fortunate, other things in life come along and they crowd out the trauma. Only in retrospect do I look back on the war and I get to feel it again. When I talk about it, see, I get teary-eyed—I can't help it. There's a lot that happened in those three years, a lot happened.

At age 94, Walter Hooke summed up his feelings about the legacy of the generation that experienced the most cataclysmic war in the history of the world for his young interviewer.

---

[35] Mr. Norton continued: 'That was real sad. Fortunately, my parents wrote me a lot, and I would write back. My father used to go down to the post office, every night, looking for the mail. He would be there waiting for a letter from me, every night, you know. The parents were concerned.'

Walter Hooke

You know, it is about the future of the world for you young people, and you have to keep everyone honest. I think that is one thing I learned with the atomic bomb, that there is no future in war, so as far as I am concerned...the worst thing that is happening is that young people are brought up to be in fear, and you should not be.

Kids should not grow up cynical—they should grow up like the world is theirs, and enjoy it and have a decent world.

Resurrection

The bell rings. The students take their seats. The lesson of the day is about to commence.

A hand shoots up.

Yes, Jessie?

Mr. Rozell, I am leaving school early on vacation and won't be here for a few days. May I have the work I will be missing?

My blood pressure ticks upward, slightly. With exams pending in the days before our Easter break, my tenth grade history student informs me that she is leaving for a vacation to Hawaii—a tad early—and she wants her assignments in advance. Since she will be missing a few classes (and she's heading to Hawaii and I am not!), I give her an extra task, never dreaming that she will actually pull it off.

Finding Randy

Randy Holmes was a couple years older than Jessie when he died. He was the first kid from our high school and all of the North Country, and quite possibly all of New York State, to be killed in World War II. Randy, you will recall, was on the *USS Oklahoma* when the Japanese torpedoed it at Pearl Harbor on December 7, 1941.

By the time I walked the halls of this high school as a student in the 1970s, no one remembered him. Today, as then, there are no plaques, no memorials on display here, outside of the local cemetery. I certainly did not know about him.

He was gone.

*

Nearly sixty years after he went missing, I've returned to the 'other side of the desk' at my alma mater. In the high school library, World War II veterans from the communities near the "Falls" have gathered on a warm spring afternoon. We're here to put on a seminar on the Pacific War for maybe a hundred excited students. During a break I'm listening to the casual conversation between our guests, and by chance I catch this snippet between Navy pilot John Leary and the Marines sitting around the table:

There was a young man from around here; he hounded his parents to let him enlist because he was only 17. Do you remember Randy Holmes?'

'Why yes, didn't the Class of 1942 dedicate their yearbook to him?'

I'm intrigued. My next step is to search the dusty yearbooks in the district vault, and sure enough, in the back of the slim 1942 volume, I find him. Randy is decked out in his white sailor's suit and cap. He is at home, on leave, crouching before some bushes in the backyard, smiling for the camera as his mother or father proudly snaps the picture. He looks happy, and proud.

And I feel like he's beckoning to me. It's similar to the picture that my father snapped of me, less than a mile away, shortly before I ventured out into the world, like Randy, for the first time.

RANDOLPH HOLMES—
MISSING IN ACTION

The photo was probably taken in the summer of 1941, after his schooling and shortly before he was assigned to the *Oklahoma*. That fall, his classmates started their senior year of high school. Everyone's world would change shortly before Christmas, and Randy would never be heard from again. His classmates would compose a final tribute to accompany the photograph:

'RANDOLPH HOLMES—MISSING IN ACTION'

'Word was received soon after the Japanese bombing of Pearl Harbor, by Mr. and Mrs. Randolph Holmes, that their son was 'missing in action.' The young sailor was on board the steamship Oklahoma, when it was struck by a Japanese bomb. Randolph would have been a member of this year's senior class if he had remained in school.

He enlisted in the Navy New Year's Day, 1941, and was sent to Newport, R.I., where he was in training as a machinist. Later he was transferred to the Great Lakes Training School in Chicago. He graduated with the rank of Seaman, Second Class.

In August of last year Randolph was ordered to report for duty to the S.S. Oklahoma. He was stationed on this boat in Pearl Harbor when the attack was made by the Japanese.

This young sailor was a popular student in Hudson Falls High School and both faculty and students keep in their hearts kind thoughts and happy memories of his manly qualities and sterling character.'

*

According to the 1940 federal census, Randy had a sister, but she left the village, as far as I can tell, becoming a nurse in the war. His parents passed away, brokenhearted. The family homestead on quiet James Street was sold. The trail just ended.

He was gone.

In the years that followed my trip to the vault, I told the story of the 'Okie' and showed my classes Randy's photograph. I would talk about him, and wonder about him. Who were his friends? How did this news affect the community? What did his death do to his parents, and his sister?

Do you realize he was your age when he died? Where is he buried? Did his body even come home?

Finally, one of my students, Mackenna, took me up on the challenge, conducted her own research, and discovered the following from the National Park Service website: 'Resting in the main channel of the harbor, a major salvage operation began in March of 1943. This massive undertaking involved the use of winches installed on Ford Island, which slowly rolled the ship back into place in an upright position. The ship was then pumped out and the remains of over 400 sailors and Marines were removed.'[60]

The remains.
Underwater.
Eighteen months.

As World War II raged on, the bodies of the men remained entombed in the ship. Parents grieved as logistics were studied and the salvage operation planned. What was left was recovered and buried in a mass grave at Pearl Harbor. Only 35 men have ever been identified.[61]

In 1947, the *Oklahoma* was sold and began its last journey to be cut up for scrap at a salvage yard in California. Not long into the journey, she began to take on water and the tow lines had to be severed; the 'Okie' slipped away into the abyss 540 miles northeast of Pearl Harbor. A former crew member summed up the feelings of many who had served aboard, and those who perished on her, when he wrote these lines:

'Good for you, Oklahoma!
Go down at sea in deep water, as you should, under the stars.
No razor blades for you!
They can make 'em from the ships and planes that did you in.
So long, Oklahoma! You were a good ship!'

The *Oklahoma* did not even have its own memorial at Pearl Harbor until 2007. But every December 7 in our school, since I found the yearbook, we make an effort in our history classes to remember the day Randy Holmes went missing.

RESURRECTION

My heart is gladdened when I arrive in school the day before the Easter holiday, open my e-mail, and find this photo.

I smile. She did it.[36]

Maybe my eyes brim for a brief instant.

Maybe Randy and all of the soldiers, sailors, and Marines and airmen are resurrected.

The kids remember.

In the words of Susie Stevens-Harvey, who lost her brother in Vietnam and advocates for all those still missing in action, or prisoners of war:

> *'Dying for freedom isn't the worst that could happen.*
> *Being forgotten is.'*

The veterans featured in this book

A SUNDAY MORNING

Harry 'Randy' Holmes: Randy was born in 1923. He and his sister lived on Rogers Street in Hudson Falls. When the author was a

---

[36] Later, after this episode has passed, I discovered that Jessie was born exactly 56 years after the day Randy died. She is a 'Pearl Harbor baby'.

kid, he would visit a neighborhood mom-and-pop grocery store on his way home from elementary school on the adjacent Maple Street. After the publication of an article related to this book, the editor of a local newspaper followed up with a note on the passing of Mrs. Nickie Piscitelli, the late owner of that store:

"1941 was Mike's Grocery's first year in business. [Following the article's publication], Nickie said that the Holmes family lived around the corner from the store. She said Randy's mother came by that day, December 7, 1941, and when the news came on the radio that the USS Oklahoma had been bombed—Nickie then pointed to where the radio had been on the shelf—Mrs. Holmes said, 'My son is on that ship!'"

As noted, Randy was killed on the *USS Oklahoma* and his remains have yet to return to his hometown to rest near his parents.

Gerald Ross: 'Barney' was born in 1921 in Whitehall, New York. He enjoyed hunting and fishing with family and was very active in community activities, especially projects and organizations related to helping veterans. He passed away at the age of 94 in 2015, a few months after this book went to press.[62]

Joseph Fiore: After the war Joe returned home and raised his family, running a liquor store and later becoming director of the Warren County Veterans Service Agency. In his civic activities, Joe Fiore worked with many veterans' organizations. He was instrumental in the establishment of the local chapter of the Marine Corps League, and with the help of many of the Marines in the book, began the annual 'Toys For Tots' Christmas drive for underprivileged children. Joe Fiore passed away in May 2015 at the age of 92.[63]

Dante Orsini: Dan became a friend of the author late in life and loved to visit with the kids in the author's classroom. Besides being in the White House Honor Guard, he also fought at Guam and Okinawa. After serving in China protecting that government against the communists immediately following the war, he was awarded the 'Order of the Cloud and Banner' by Chiang Kai-shek himself. He served his community in many ways up until the week before he passed in 2013 at age 93.[64]

THE DEFENDERS/ CAPTIVITY

Joseph Minder: Joe Minder's POW experiences as recorded in his diary form the backdrop of this work; the bulk of it is published here for the first time. He kept his notes on cigarette paper and other scraps and managed to keep them hidden from his captors. Joe sent the author a typewritten copy of his diary in the late 1990s, and it was reformatted in the spring semester of 2015 for use here by the author's students as a class project. Joe was repatriated and returned home to North Creek, New York, marrying and raising 2 sons and working for the local garnet mine. He became an expert ski instructor in the fledgling downhill skiing industry. Joe Minder passed away in 2006 at the age of 88.[65]

Richard M. Gordon: Major Gordon retired from the U.S. Army and became one of the founding members of the 'Battling Bastards of Bataan,' an organization committed to honoring the memory of the soldiers of the Philippines and to educating future generations. He led many tours back to the authentic sites and helped erect several monuments to the fallen. Major Gordon passed away in 2003 at the age of 81.[66]

John Parsons: John Parsons, having survived the Bataan Death March, gave an interview to the local newspaper in 1946 recounting his experiences. At Mukden POW camp in Manchuria, he was subjected to beatings and starvation. The Japanese also conducted a secret program that included bacteriological experiments, which the Japanese and American governments today do not acknowledge. Parsons was liberated by the Red Army on August 20, 1945. He suffered greatly from his wartime experiences, and owing to a lack of 'documentation' at the hands of his captors, he was denied full disability benefits by the U.S. Government, not an uncommon occurrence for POWs. He passed away in 1965 at the age of 53, having been bedridden for the previous five years.[67]

INTO THE FRAY

Dorothy Schechter: Dorothy Schechter was born in 1919 in eastern Pennsylvania. She attended Pennsylvania State University and married in 1941 before the war broke out. Mrs. Schechter, a civilian, was working at various bases in the United States because her husband, in military intelligence, was frequently on the move. After the war, she went with her husband Joe to Europe where he attempted to find members of his Jewish family in Poland and Austria, but they had all been murdered in the Holocaust. Soon after returning, Joe was diagnosed with a genetic disorder and passed away a few years later, at the age of 39. Mrs. Schechter was just 34, but never remarried. After his passing, she worked for a law firm and became a tax attorney before retiring. Mrs. Schechter loved reading and travel and her beloved dachshund was a constant companion.[68]

John A. Leary: Judge Leary was a recipient of the Navy Cross and married while in the service during World War II. He returned from the war and earned a degree in law, setting up practice in Hudson Falls, New York. He later served as Washington County Court judge and district attorney with an illustrious career of public and civil service. He passed away in 2003 at the age of 84. For most of his life he loved flying, and his original flightlog and various maps and photographs from the campaign against Rabaul and other targets can be seen at bit.ly/LearyGallery.[69]

A TURNING POINT/GUADALCANAL

Robert Addison: Bob Addison served as the first Director of Athletics at Adirondack Community College and later became a full-time professor and beloved coach. He enjoyed attending reunions of Edson's Raiders long after the war with his friend Gerry West. He passed away in 2013 at the age of 90.[70]

Gerald West: Gerry West was a life member and past president of the Edson's Raiders Association. He served in Korea and later joined the U.S. Army after his time in the Marine Corps. He had a career in retail, where he ran into Bob Addison again in 1962, recognizing him as he was selling him kitchen appliances. Gerry West passed away in 2014 at the age of 95. Before their passing, the author was instrumental in helping the New York State Senate to induct Gerry West and Bob Addison jointly into the Senate Veterans Hall of Fame in May 2013..[71]

Thomas H. Jones: Tom Jones was born in 1913, in Wilkes Barre, Pennsylvania. Orphaned early in life, he served in the U.S. Marine Corps from 1931 to 1935, then again during World War II in the South Pacific with First Marine Division at Guadalcanal, Cape Gloucester, and Peleliu, where he received the Purple Heart. In retirement, he enjoyed fly fishing with his own tied flies in the Adirondacks. He was 99 years old when he passed away in 2013, and wished to be remembered as a proud Marine and true gentleman.[72]

SEA ACTION/THE KAMIKAZES

Alvin Peachman: Mr. Peachman taught history for over thirty years after returning from the war and getting his teaching credentials. He lived in the small house where he raised his family near the high school where we both taught, and spent his winters in Hawaii, which he was introduced to in World War II and where he and his late wife had many friends. At 96 he could still be seen taking his daily walks and talking to the people he met and could still instantly recall the names of students he had in class nearly 60 years previously, upon encountering them. Mr. Peachman passed in November 2020 at the age of 98, five years after the original publication of this book.[73]

ISLANDS OF THE DAMNED

Ralph Leinoff: After the war, Ralph married and raised two sons with his wife. He worked as a salesman and graphic designer. Ralph also spent 27 years in the service of the New York City Fire Department. He was a consummate artist and raconteur throughout his life, expressing himself in painting, pencilwork, ceramics, videography, sculpture, acrylics, lyrics, and composition. Mr. and Mrs. Leinoff supported many community causes. They also pursued a host of other interests, including world travel and community service and patronage. Ralph became close to several of the author's student interviewers, even buying their textbooks for their college pursuits. He passed away in 2014 at the age of 91.[74]

Walter Hooke: Walter Hooke was born in 1913 and joined the Marine Corps in 1942. Serving in Nagasaki with the occupation forces solidified a passion to work for peace. He became close to the Catholic Bishop of Nagasaki, Paul Yamaguchi, and upon returning home, became a vocal advocate for the National Association of Radiation Survivors. He was also instrumental in lobbying legislators for benefits for the Atomic War Veterans; he thought the decision to use the atomic bombs had been misguided and wrong. He passed away in 2010 at the age of 97. An admirer noted on his passing, *"I regret that I shall not hear again, Walter's intoning on the answering machine, 'Have a gentle day.' "*[75]

Nicholas Grinaldo: For his actions on Saipan, Nick Grinaldo received the Bronze Star. He was honorably discharged in 1945 with the rank of staff sergeant. After the war Nick returned to Troy, New York, where he operated Nick's Shoe Store, a store that was first opened in 1917 by his uncle. He enjoyed time with his family and was active in many civic organizations. He passed away in 2012 at the age of 92.[76]

John Sidur: Due to the fact that he was treated by a Marine corpsman on Saipan and not an Army doctor and the subsequent confusion and loss of records, John Sidur was denied a Purple Heart for his actions on Saipan, but would receive one for suffering a wound at Okinawa—very belatedly—in a special ceremony in 2010, 65 years after that battle. 'It almost makes me cry,' he said at the time. 'It's a long time coming.' He passed away in 2015 at the age of 97.[77]

Daniel Lawler: Dan Lawler was a frequent visitor to the author's classroom, bringing his Marine scrapbook and various souvenirs and funny stories from his time in Okinawa, Peleliu, and China as a member of the First Marine Division K/3/5. He was awarded the Purple Heart, which he highly treasured. While in K Company, Dan was honored to serve with future author Eugene B.

Sledge, whose book, *With The Old Breed*, captured the experiences of the Pacific battlefield. Other Marine brothers of the company included Sen. Paul Douglas of Illinois, who Dan visited in Washington after the war. Dan passed away at the age of 90 in September 2015.[78]

John Murray: John Murray, severely wounded at Peleliu, was evacuated and later awarded the Purple Heart at a hospital in San Diego. Through his life he remained close to his Marine buddies in this book, notably Jim Butterfield and Dan Lawler. Like many veterans, he raised his family but did not speak about his wartime experiences. His account here in this book was written in a 1995 letter to his son, which was shared with the author after he died. He passed away in 1998.[79]

James and Mary Butterfield: As noted, Jim and Mary were high school sweethearts who married soon after the war, despite Jim having been blinded for life in May 1945 at Okinawa. After the war, Jim endured many reconstructive surgeries on his face but overcame his disability, and he and Mary became the proud owners of Butterfield's Grocery Store on Bay St. in Glens Falls, New York, for 40 years. It was said that Mr. Butterfield could tell the denomination of the bill that was handed to him by its texture and touch. They loved traveling to Hawaii and Florida; Jim particularly enjoyed needling the Japanese tourists and businessmen he encountered in Hawaii, joking that the sniper who shot him on Okinawa probably owned a hotel in Honolulu. They were married for 67 years and cherished the time spent with their family. Mary passed in October 2012; Jim passed the following summer at the age of 87.[80]

CAPTIVITY—YEAR 3: THE HELLSHIPS

Robert Blakeslee: Hellship sinking survivor Robert Blakeslee passed away in 1976. His daughter Nancy Blakeslee Wood recently discovered a collection of her mother's letters, which were always marked 'Returned to Sender,' and also his postcards, which amounted to a short checklist regarding his health status and what he could receive from her in the camps, but never did.[81]

THE SANDS OF IWO JIMA

Sanford Berkman: Sandy was born in Cohoes, New York, in 1920. After the war, Sandy was the owner and operator of Kaye's Catering, a business he ran with his wife. After his career in the catering business, Sandy worked for the Commissioner of Jurors in Albany for many years until his retirement. He passed away in 2017 at the age of 97.[82]

Arthur Laporte: Art LaPorte was interviewed on many occasions for this project, both at his home and at classroom symposiums. Like many World War II veterans, LaPorte would go on to serve in Korea, sustaining additional wounds there; he was not shy about rolling up his pants leg or sleeve to show students where chunks of muscle were missing, though that did not stop him from working hard at the mill and literally digging his own basement by hand with a shovel after the war. Like many veterans, he still can recite how to field strip/clean his weapon, memorizing the parts and the sequence, decades after combat. Art passed away at 93 on August 15, 2019; I thought he would never die. I shared this sentiment with one of my former students who sent me the notice of his passing, and she responded, '*My childhood was spent living right next door to him on Pine Street. He was always larger than life to me, and I never understood him. He had a crow named Junior that he would holler to every morning, and it would come and land on his shoulder and walk around the yard with him. He had howling coyote dogs as pets, Buffy and Shadow. A man of few words and weathered hands which I always knew had a story behind them as a child. To say that I was blown away when he ever walked into the classroom and spoke of his story would be an understatement. He certainly was a soul like no other.*'[83]

Herbert Altshuler: Herb and his wife retired to the North Country by the 'Falls' after a successful career. He enjoyed giving freely of his time to our high school students and was interviewed on several occasions, and maintained relationships with them after the interviews were over. They are always in the audience when the author gives a lecture or slideshow locally.[84]

Walter Hammer: Walter Hammer was born in 1924, and along with the other Marines in this book, was a frequent contributor to the panel discussions set up by the author at his high school. Nicknamed 'Sledge' by his buddies, Walt went on to receive the Silver Star for his brave actions under fire at Iwo Jima, which he never brought up in our panel discussions with the students. He passed away in 2008 at the age of 83.

A RAIN OF RUIN

Andy Doty: After the war, Andy Doty married his high school sweetheart, Eleanor Baker, the daughter of the local druggist, and raised three girls, settling in Palo Alto, California, and retiring as Director of Community Affairs for Stanford University. You can read more about his World War II experiences in my second book *War in the Air* or by searching for his out-of-print 1995 memoir with the information provided in the 'Source Notes' in the back of this book.[85]

TYPHOON OF STEEL/OKINAWA

Bruce Manell: Bruce Manell enjoyed a storied career in area law enforcement, retiring as Deputy Chief of Police in the Hudson Falls Police Department. He loved photography and bowling and wrote a column for the local newspaper on the bowling leagues. He passed away in 2009.[86]

Katherine Abbott: Kay Abbot was born in 1917 in Glens Falls, New York, and received her training as a registered nurse at Albany Memorial Hospital. Along with her five brothers, she served in the U.S. Army during World War II. While serving in the Army, Kay was a flight nurse and would help many soldiers on the flights from the Philippines to Hawaii and San Francisco. After the service, Kay worked for Albany Veterans Hospital as an RN, retiring in 1980. She was an active member of the World War II Flight Nurses

THE THINGS OUR FATHERS SAW (VOL. I) | 269

Association, and really enjoyed their reunions. She was also a charter member of the World War II Memorial Society. She passed in December 2007 at the age of 90.[87]

REDEMPTION

John Norton: Mr. Norton returned home from sea in 1946. He became involved in local politics and civic organizations, and later served as the mayor of Granville, New York. Near the occasion of his 99th birthday, John summed up his love of his small hometown, typical of many of our hometown World War II veterans. 'When I joined the Navy, I wanted to get the hell out of Granville. But once I did, I couldn't wait to get back. I met fellows from all over the country, but never met anyone like Granville people.' [88]

Joseph Marcino: Joe Marcino joined the Marines after graduating from Whitehall High School and was awarded the Bronze Star for bravery under fire at the battle of Iwo Jima. He went on to become a celebrated and much-loved football coach and athletic director. He passed away in 2014 at the age of 91.[89]

****

IF YOU LIKED THIS BOOK, you'll love hearing more from the World War II generation in my other books. On the following pages you can see some samples, and I can let you know as soon as the new books are out and offer you exclusive discounts on some material. Just sign up at matthewrozellbooks.com

Some of my readers may like to know that all of my books are **directly available from the author, with collector's sets which can be autographed** in paperback and hardcover. They are popular gifts for that 'hard-to-buy-for' guy or gal on your list.

Visit my shop at matthewrozellbooks.com for details.

Thank you for reading!

I hope you found this book interesting and informative; I sure learned a lot researching and writing it. What follows are some descriptions of my other books.

Find them all at <u>matthewrozellbooks.com.</u>

The Things Our Fathers Saw—The Untold Stories of the World War II Generation-Volume II: War in the Air—From the Great Depression to Combat 320 pages.

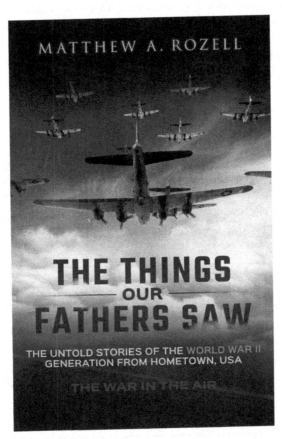

—FROM THE BOOK—

— "You flew with what I would call 'controlled fear.' You were scared stiff, but it was controlled. My ball turret gunner—he couldn't take it anymore... I guess he was right. He's dead now. But he had lost control of the fear. He never got out of that ball turret; he died in that ball turret." —B-24 BOMBARDIER

— "I spent a lot of time in hospitals. I had a lot of trouble reconciling how my mother died [of a cerebral hemorrhage] from the telegram she opened, saying I was [shot down and] 'missing in action.' I didn't explain to her the fact that 'missing in action' is not necessarily 'killed in action.' You know? I didn't even think about that. How do you think you feel when you find out you killed your mother?" —B-24 BOMBARDIER

— "I was in the hospital with a flak wound. The next mission, the entire crew was killed. The thing that haunts me is that I can't put a face to the guy who was a replacement. He was an eighteen-year-old Jewish kid named Henry Vogelstein from Brooklyn. It was his first and last mission. He made his only mission with a crew of strangers." —B-24 NAVIGATOR

— "The German fighters picked us. I told the guys, 'Keep your eyes open, we are about to be hit!' I saw about six or eight feet go off my left wing. I rang the 'bail-out' signal, and I reached out and grabbed the co-pilot out of his seat. I felt the airplane climbing, and I thought to myself, 'If this thing stalls out, and starts falling down backwards, no one is going to get out...'" — B-17 PILOT

My BEST 4 FRIENDS of our Crew all Killed in action But me

—"I get a little emotional. I'm almost 93; I hope to see them all again in heaven."— B-17 TAIL GUNNER

The Things Our Fathers Saw—The Untold Stories of the World War II Generation-Volume III: War in the Air—Combat, Captivity, and Reunion

Volume 3 is about the Air War again, and this time I have some of my friends who were fighter pilots, including a Tuskegee Airman who had to deal with racism back home, on top of defeating fascism in Europe. There is also the story of my B-17 crew friends, sitting around a table and telling about the day they were all shot down over Germany, and how they survived the prisoner-of-war experience in the last year of the war.

—"After the first mission Colonel Davis told us, 'From now on you are going to go with the bombers all the way through the mission to the target.' It didn't always work, but that was our mission—we kept the Germans off the bombers. At first they didn't want us, but toward the end, they started asking for us as an escort, because we protected them to and from the missions." —**Tuskegee Airman, WWII**

— "[Someone in the PoW camp] said, 'Look down there at the main gate!', and the American flag was flying! We went berserk, we just went berserk! We were looking at the goon tower and there's no goons there, there are Americans up there! And we saw the American flag, I mean—to this day I start to well up when I see the flag." —**Former prisoner of war, WWII**

— "I got back into my turret. Fellas, the turret wasn't there anymore. That German fighter who had been eyeing me came in and he hit his 20mm gun, took the top of that Plexiglas and tore it right off! Now we're defenseless. The planes ahead of us have been shot down, we're lumbering along at 180 miles an hour, and these fighters were just [warming up] for target practice." —**B-17 Turret Gunner**

The Things Our Fathers Saw—The Untold Stories of the World War II Generation-Volume IV: 'Up the Bloody Boot'—The War in Italy

Volume 4 in this series will take you from the deserts of North Africa to the mountains of Italy with the men and women veterans of the Italian campaign who open up about a war that was so brutal, news of it was downplayed at home. The war in the Mediterranean, and particularly the Italian Campaign, is one that for many Americans is shrouded in mystery and murkiness. Yet it was here that the United States launched its first offensive in the west on enemy soil, and it was here that Allied forces would be slogging it out with a tenacious enemy fighting for its life in the longest single American Campaign of World War II.

—*"There was an old French fort there, and we could look down on it during the day. We gauged the way we would hit that place so that the moon would set right between two mountain peaks; we timed it so when we got there, that moon would silhouette them, but not us... We carried out the first and only bayonet charge [of the war] by our Rangers; we didn't fire; very few people knew that we carried out an overnight bayonet attack. I'll tell you, that's something. You see that, it'll shake you up real good." —U.S. Army Ranger, WWII*

— *"We attacked another hill, and I shot a German soldier. And then the Germans counterattacked on the hill, and I could not escape, so I decided to just lay down on top of that soldier and make believe I'm dead. They passed me by, I got up and [this German I shot] starts talking to me in English, he says he's from Coney Island, in Brooklyn; he went to visit his mother in Germany and they put him in the army. And he was dying, and he says to me, 'You can take my cigarettes; you can take my schnapps.' Then he died right underneath me. And I imagine he knew I had shot him...."*
—*U.S. Army scout, WWII*

— "So there was a terrific fight going on in a place called Santa Maria, south of Rome. While we were going through, in transit, we stopped at a big Italian barn; they had a kitchen set up, and we had our own mess kits. As we were going through the line, we saw this huge rack of shelves with American Army duffel bags packed on there. And Hendrickson said to me, 'Hey, Tony, you know what? My brother must be in the area someplace. There's his duffel bag.' The name was stenciled on. So I said, 'That's nice.' [But] I was thinking, why is his duffel bag there? Well, there was a military policeman guarding these bags. I went back to the MP. I said to him, 'What are these bags doing here?' And I told him about Hendrickson. 'Well,' he said, 'I don't know if you want to tell him, but these guys are all dead. They were all killed at Santa Maria.'" —**U.S. Army map maker, WWII**

The Things Our Fathers Saw—The Untold Stories of the World War II Generation-Volume V: 'D-Day and Beyond'—The War in France

Volume 5 in this series will take you from the bloody beach at Omaha through the hedgerow country of Normandy and beyond, American veterans of World War II--Army engineers and infantrymen, Coast Guardsmen and Navy sailors, tank gunners and glider pilots--sit down with you across the kitchen table and talk about what they saw and experienced, tales they may have never told anyone before.

— *"I had a vision, if you want to call it that. At my home, the mailman would walk up towards the front porch, and I saw it just as clear as if he's standing beside me—I see his blue jacket and the blue cap and the leather mailbag. Here he goes up to the house, but he doesn't turn. He goes right up the front steps.*

This happened so fast, probably a matter of seconds, but the first thing that came to mind, that's the way my folks would find out what happened to me.

The next thing I know, I kind of come to, and I'm in the push-up mode. I'm half up out of the underwater depression, and I'm trying to figure out what the hell happened to those prone figures on the beach, and all of a sudden, I realized I'm in amongst those bodies!" —Army demolition engineer, Omaha Beach, D-Day

— *"My last mission was the Bastogne mission. We were being towed, we're approaching Bastogne, and I see a cloud of flak, anti-aircraft fire. I said to myself, 'I'm not going to make it.' There were a couple of groups ahead of us, so now the anti-aircraft batteries are zeroing in. Every time a new group came over, they kept zeroing in. My outfit had, I think, 95% casualties." —Glider pilot, D-Day and Beyond*

— *"I was fighting in the hedgerows for five days; it was murder. But psychologically, we were the best troops in the world. There was nobody like us; I had all the training that they could give us, but nothing prepares you for some things.*

You know, in my platoon, the assistant platoon leader got shot right through the head, right through the helmet, dead, right there in front of me. That affects you, doesn't it?" —Paratrooper, D-Day and Beyond

~SOON TO BE A DOCUMENTARY MINI-SERIES~

THE HOLOCAUST was a watershed event in history. In this book, Matthew Rozell reconstructs a lost chapter—the liberation of a 'death train' deep in the heart of Nazi Germany in the closing days of World War II. Drawing on never-before published eye-witness accounts, survivor testimony, and wartime reports and letters, Rozell brings to life the incredible true stories behind the iconic 1945 liberation photographs taken by the soldiers who were there. He weaves together a chronology of the Holocaust as it unfolds across Europe, and goes back to literally retrace the steps of the survivors and the American soldiers who freed them. Rozell's work results in joyful reunions on three continents, seven decades later. He offers his unique perspective on the lessons of the Holocaust for future generations, and the impact that one person can make.

A selection of comments left by reviewers:

"**Extraordinary research** into an event which needed to be told. I have read many books about the Holocaust and visited various museums but had not heard reference to this train previously. The fact that people involved were able to connect, support and help heal each other emotionally was amazing."

"**The story of the end of the Holocaust and the Nazi regime** told from a very different and precise angle. First-hand accounts from Jewish survivors and the US soldiers that secured their freedom. Gripping."

"**Mr. Rozell travels 'back to the future'** of people who were not promised a tomorrow; neither the prisoners nor the troops knew what horrors the next moment would bring. He captures the parallel experience of soldiers fighting ruthless Nazism and the ruthless treatment of Jewish prisoners."

"**If you have any trepidation** about reading a book on the Holocaust, this review is for you. [Matthew Rozell] masterfully conveys the individual stories of those featured in the book in a manner that does not leave the reader with a sense of despair, but rather a sense of purpose."

"**Could not put this book down**--I just finished reading *A Train Near Magdeburg*. Tears fell as I read pages and I smiled through others. I wish I could articulate the emotions that accompanied me through the stories of these beautiful people."

"**Everyone should read this book**, detailing the amazing bond that formed between Holocaust survivors likely on their way to death in one last concentration camp as WWII was about to end, and a small number of American soldiers that happened upon the stopped train and liberated the victims. The lifelong friendships that resulted between the survivors and their liberators is a testament to compassion and goodness. It is amazing that the author is not Jewish but a "reluctant" history teacher who ultimately becomes a Holocaust scholar. This is a great book."

ABOUT THE AUTHOR

Photo Credit: Kris Dressen, SUNY Geneseo.

Matthew Rozell is an award-winning history teacher, author, speaker, and blogger on the topic of the most cataclysmic events in the history of mankind-World War II and the Holocaust. Rozell has been featured as the "ABC World News Person of the Week" and has had his work as a teacher filmed for the CBS Evening News, NBC Learn, the Israeli Broadcast Authority, the United States Holocaust Memorial Museum, and the New York State United Teachers. He writes on the power of teaching and the importance of the study of history at <u>TeachingHistoryMatters.com,</u> and you can 'Like' his Facebook author page at <u>MatthewRozellBooks</u> for updates.

About this Book/ Acknowledgements

This book has been a nascent dream for over twenty years.

As I write this, it is very early morning before I head off to school to teach young people for the day—and this is what I have been doing nearly all of my adult life.

When someone asked former teacher Frank McCourt why it took him so long to finally write his runaway memoir *Angela's Ashes* at age sixty-six, he replied, "Well, I was busy teaching school."

So it is.

*

A note on historiographical style and convention: to enhance accuracy, consistency, and readability, I corrected punctuation and spelling and sometimes even place names, but only after extensive research. I did take the liberty of occasionally condensing the speaker's voice, eliminating side tangents or incidental information not relevant to the matter at hand. Sometimes two or more of our original interviews with the same person were combined for readability and narrative flow. All of the words of the subjects, however, are essentially their own.

Additionally, I chose to utilize endnotes where I deemed them appropriate, directing readers who wish to learn more to my sources, notes, and side commentary. I hope that they do not detract from the flow of the narrative.

First, I wish to acknowledge the hundreds of students who passed through my classes and who forged the bonds with the World War II generation. I promised you this book someday, and now that many of you are yourselves parents, you can tell your children this book is for them. Who says young people are indifferent to the past? Here is evidence to the contrary.

The Hudson Falls Central School District and my colleagues have my deep appreciation for supporting this endeavor and recognizing its significance throughout the years.

Jeanne Winston Alder, author, and the editor of the most important collection of Revolutionary War veteran oral histories perhaps in all of New York State, first recognized the potential and showed special interest in this project and edited three of my articles which first appeared in the *Journal of the Washington County Historical Society*. Those articles became the genesis of this book.

Several people read and commented on the original manuscript. For helpful feedback and suggestions I am indebted to Sunny Buchman, Alan Bush, Joseph Cutshall-King, Donna Payne Hughes, Mary Murray, and Pauline Kolman Rosenberg. Cara Quinlan's sharp eyes and ears caught errors that were missed in an earlier edition. My wife Laura also provided some early feedback. Additionally, Sunny Buchman was one of my early champions and worked to arrange interviews with the folks at her retirement community, The Glen at Hiland Meadows. My good friend Susan Winchell took time out of her busy schedule to put her remarkable talents to work to get the maps just the way I needed them. My friend Rob Miller traveled to my hometown to take some very special portraits of our veterans and participate in some of our events recognizing them. Todd DeGarmo of the Folklife Center at Crandall Public Library in

Glens Falls found information from the 1940 census on Randy Holmes' family, and also helped with background information on the *LOOK Magazine* series that profiled the Glens Falls–North Country region as "Hometown, USA" during the war. Stephen Blakeslee sent me his father's 1945 narrative when I called for stories back in the late 1990s, and it was the inspiration for the chapter on the hellships. Daniel Leary provided unrestricted access to his father's flight log, photographs, and documents, and Judge Leary's family provided early financial support for this history project. John Murray entrusted me with his late father's writings, and Ron Parsons gave me ongoing support and the background of his father's POW ordeal, clarifying the picture of how, for many former prisoners, the battles did not end with the war. The Minder family was also supportive, and I think happy that Joseph Minder's war diary will now be appreciated by a wider audience. I hope that I did Joe some small measure of justice.

Naturally this work would not have been possible had it not been for the willingness of the veterans to share their stories for posterity. Andy Doty graciously allowed me to use excerpts from his well-written war autobiography. All of the veterans who were interviewed for this book had the foresight to complete release forms granting me access to their stories, and for us to share the information with the New York State Military Museum's Veterans Oral History Project, where copies of most of the interviews reside. As of this writing, fully ten percent of the 600 videos recently uploaded to the NYSMM's YouTube channel were interviews conducted by me or my students, and Wayne Clarke and Mike Russert of the NYSMMVOP were instrumental in cultivating this relationship with my classes over the years. Additionally, James Gandy, the assistant librarian and archivist at the NYSMM, helped secure materials related to the 27th Infantry Division on Saipan. Chris Carola of the Associated Press, as always, was supportive and uncovered

NOTES

A Sunday Morning

The chapter title was inspired by a heading in Studs Terkel's Pulitzer Prize winning The Good War: An Oral History of World War II (1984), undoubtedly the primary influence on my career in narrative history and on this work.

Map, *'Extent of Japanese Control in the Pacific, 1942'* by Susan Winchell-Sweeney, Matthew Rozell, Editor [2015] after Donald L. Miller, *The Story of World War II.* New York: Simon & Schuster, 2001. Digital data sources: Esri, HERE, Delorme, USGS, Intermap, increment P Corp., NRCAN, Esri Japan, METI, Esri China (Hong Kong), Esri (Thailand), TomTom, MapmyIndia, OpenStreetMap contributors, and the GIS User Community.

[1] Testimony of Stephen Bower Young, cited in Miller, Donald. *The Story of World War II.* New York: Simon & Schuster, 2001. 90. In this work, I have leaned heavily on Donald L. Miller. I had searched for months for a good 'textbook' to use with high school seniors. In addition to Terkel, mentioned above, this book fit the bill and I have used it in the classroom for over a decade.

[2] After Action Report. USS Oklahoma, Reports of Pearl Harbor Attack. 20 December 1941. Department of the Navy-Navy Historical Center.

[3] "World War II-Valor in the Pacific National Monument". National Park Service, U.S. Department of the Interior. http://www.nps.gov/valr/index.htm.

[4] Morton, Louis. *The Fall of the Philippines, Chapter V: The First Days of War.* CMH Pub 5-2. US Army Center for Military

History. 1953. www.history.army.mil/books/wwii/5-2/5-2_5.htm

THE DEFENDERS

Map, *'Route of Pvt. Joseph G. Minder in the Philippines, Oct. 1941-May 1942.'* by Susan Winchell Sweeney, Matthew Rozell, Editor [2015]. Digital data sources: Esri, HERE, Delorme, USGS, Intermap, increment P Corp., NRCAN, Esri Japan, METI, Esri China (Hong Kong), Esri (Thailand), TomTom, MapmyIndia, OpenStreetMap contributors, and the GIS User Community.

[5] Tenney, Lester I. *My Hitch in Hell: the Bataan Death March.* London: Brassey's, 2001. 38. Lester Tenney, a Bataan Death March survivor and POW slave laborer at a mine in Japan, filed a pioneering lawsuit against the Japanese company he slaved for while a POW in Japan. In 2000, it was dismissed in a California court at the urging of the U.S. Government. In 2003, the U.S. Supreme Court turned aside this case and dozens of other POW slave labor claims.

[6] "Malinta Tunnel." Corregidor: The Island Fortress. http://www.corregidorisland.com/malinta.html.

[7] Ward, Geoffrey C. and Burns, Ken. *The War- An Intimate History.* New York: Alfred. A. Knopf, 2007.38.

[8] Miller, *The Story of World War II.* 105,111.

[9] Burr, Patten. "John Parsons, Local GI, Recounts Jap Tortures", *The Glens Falls Post-Star,* Jan. 30, 1946.

[10] Sloan, Bill. "Corregidor: The Last Battle in the Fall of the Philippines." HistoryNet. http://www.historynet.com/corregidor-the-last-battle-in-the-fall-of-the-philippines.htm.

[11] "Defenders of the Philippines." *92nd Garage Area.* http://philippine-defenders.lib.wv.us/html/92nd_garage.html.

[12] "Defenders" of the Philippines." *Cabanatuan.* http://philippine-defenders.lib.wv.us/html/cabanatuan.html

[13] Holmes, Linda Goetz. *Unjust Enrichment: How Japan's Companies Built Postwar Fortunes Using American POWs.* Mechanicsburg, PA: Stackpole Books, 2001. 13.

[14] Miller, *The Story of World War II.* 125.

[15] Keegan, John. *The Second World War*. New York: Viking, 1990. 275.

A TURNING POINT/GUADALCANAL

Map, *'Guadalcanal, Sept. 1942'* by Susan Winchell-Sweeney, Matthew Rozell, Editor [2015], after Hoffman, Major Jon T., *From Makin to Bougainville: Marine Raiders in the Pacific War*. National Park Service website. Digital data sources: Esri, HERE, Delorme, USGS, Intermap, increment P Corp., NRCAN, Esri Japan, METI, Esri China (Hong Kong), Esri (Thailand), TomTom, MapmyIndia, OpenStreetMap contributors, and the GIS User Community.

[16] Ward, Geoffrey C. and Burns, Ken. *The War*, 49.
[17] Alexander, Colonel Joseph H. *Edson's Raiders: The First Marine Raider Battalion in World War II*. Annapolis: Naval Institute Press, 2000. 49.
[18] Alexander, *Edson's Raiders*. 32.
[19] Alexander, *Edson's Raiders*. 60-63
[20] Alexander, *Edson's Raiders*. 102.
[21] Mr. Jones continued: "Matter of fact, he wanted me to stay out there and work for them. One day, he came to me and said— they were high society— he said, 'There's going to be a debutante coming-out party. We always like to have a few service men present, so it doesn't look too bad.' He asked if I would go with his friend's daughter. I said yes. He said it wasn't a romance or anything. I told him I would accompany her. Her name was Anne Folger, the coffee people, from Folgers coffee. Anyway, they took pictures of this coming-out party, and that's one of the pictures that was in *LIFE Magazine*... [*shows clipping*] That's me with Anne Folger... At the table were the Spreckles, they were the big sugar people [on the west coast]. One of them was married to Clark Gable, the movie actor. I was in way over my head.... Incidentally, you don't remember the Mansons, do you? How his people murdered Sharon Tate, and Anne Folger...she was one of the girls that they murdered!"
[22] Alexander, *Edson's Raiders*. 112-115.

[23] Alexander, *Edson's Raiders.* 153.

[24] Miller, *The Story of World War II.* 151.

[25] Manchester, William. *Goodbye, Darkness: A Memoir of the Pacific War* (Boston: Little, Brown) 1987. p. 175, 209.

[26] I asked Gerry West, of Washington County, New York, how fellow Raider Bob Addison, originally from Ohio, came to be reacquainted with him. "Well, the funny thing was, after I retired from the military in March of '62, that summer Bob got transferred in [to work at the fledging Adirondack Community College] and came into Sears [store where Gerry worked] to buy his appliances. He looked over at me and walked over and said, 'I know you from somewhere.' I knew the face, and I mean you're talking twenty years, because the last time I had seen Bob was in 1943 in Camp Elliott. So it was like 19 years later! We got talking, and the minute he said, 'Marine Corps,' then I remembered."

[27] Wagner, Richard. *Richard Wagner War Diary* cited in Larson, Don, *Lucky's Life.* 2014. Privately published.

SEA ACTION

[28] Interview with Alvin Peachman, June 16, 2003.

CAPTIVITY—YEAR 2

Source: Minder, Joseph G. *World War II Diary of Joseph G. Minder, 1941-1945.*

[29] Burr, Patten. "John Parsons, Local GI, Recounts Jap Tortures", *The Glens Falls Post-Star,* Jan. 30, 1946.

[30] Supplemental information from "Memorial Day- Three Wars, Three Vets Remember". *Writings From Main Street,* https://dadoonan.wordpress.com, May 17, 2007.

ISLANDS OF THE DAMNED

The chapter title was inspired by R.V. Burgin's World War II Marine memoir of the same name.

[31] Berry, Henry. *Semper Fi, Mac: Living Memories of the U.S. Marines in World War II.* New York: Arbor House, 1982.

[32] Carola, Chris. "US Survivors of WWII Battle Recall Saipan Attack." *Associated Press.* July 6, 2014.

[33] O'Brien, Francis. *Battling For Saipan.* New York: Ballantine Books, 2003. xi.

[34] Carola, Chris. "US Survivors of WWII Battle Recall Saipan Attack." *Associated Press.* July 6, 2014.

[35] Miller, *The Story of World War II.* 379.

[36] Hough, Frank O. *The Seizure of Peleliu.* USMC Historical Monograph. Historical Branch, G-3 Division, Headquarters, U.S. Marine Corps. 94.

[37] A *Glens Falls Post-Star* clipping dated Jan. 13, 1945, indicates Mr. Murray was wounded at 'Palau Island in the South Pacific area.' This is technically incorrect, but not surprising. Little was known about the battle for Peleliu back home at the time it was being fought, and it was soon overshadowed by larger campaigns. Hearing the division commander's pronouncement that the operation would take three days at the most, few of the press corps were on the scene, many opting to travel with MacArthur to the long-awaited re-conquest of the Philippines. John's narrative has been excerpted from a private account written in 1995.

[38] Taken from a series of classroom interviews with Dan Lawler and James Butterfield over several years, beginning in May 2000.

CAPTIVITY—YEAR 3: THE HELLSHIPS

[39] "Defenders of the Philippines." Hellships. http://philippine-defenders.lib.wv.us/html/hellships.html.

[40] Blakeslee, Robert B. Unpublished interview conducted in 1945.

[41] Burr, Patten. "John Parsons, Local GI, Recounts Jap Tortures", *The Glens Falls Post-Star,* Jan. 30, 1946.

THE SANDS OF IWO JIMA

The chapter title was inspired by the famous film of the same name.
[42] *World War II: Time-Life Books History of the Second World War.* New York: Prentice Hall, 1989.

CAPTIVITY—YEAR 4: THE COPPER MINE

Source: Minder, Joseph G. *World War II Diary of Joseph G. Minder, 1941-1945.*
This particular mine was owned by the Kajima Corporation. "Working conditions were dangerous and mistreatment a daily occurrence. Most slave labor was for the Fujita-gumi Construction Company." Source: "Hanaoka Sendai #7-B", *Center for Research, Allied POWS Under the Japanese.*
www.mansell.com/pow_resources/camplists/sendai/sendai_07_hanuoka/hanaoka_7_b.html.

A RAIN OF RUIN

The chapter title is inspired by President Harry S. Truman's Aug. 6, 1945, admonition that the Japanese would face a "rain of ruin from the air" if they did not surrender.
[43] Miller, *The Story of World War II.* 441,448.
[44] Miller, *The Story of World War II.* 458-61.

THE KAMIKAZES

[45] "MacArthur's Speeches: Radio Message from the Leyte Beachhead", *American Experience: MacArthur*
www.pbs.org/wgbh/amex/macarthur/filmmore/reference/primary/macspeech03.html
[46] Miller, *The Story of World War II.* 415.
[47] Miller, *The Story of World War II.* 416.
[48] Crossing the 'T' illustration, Stephan Brunker 2004. Courtesy Wikimedia Commons.

TYPHOON OF STEEL/OKINAWA

[49]Interview with Bruce Manell. Interviewed by Kayla Cronin, Dec. 18, 2003.
[50]Interview with James Butterfield. Interviewed by Matthew Rozell, Veterans' Symposium, May 29, 2001. Sara Prehoda and Jackie Quarters helped with the transcription.
[51]Classroom interview with Dan Lawler and James Butterfield. Interviewed by Matthew Rozell, Nov. 24, 2003.
[52]Sloan, Bill, *The Ultimate Battle −Okinawa 1945 −The Last Epic Battle of World War II.* New York: Simon & Schuster. 2007. 257.
[53] This segment was taken from a classroom interview with Dan Lawler, James Butterfield, and Mary Butterfield on Jan. 11, 2007. Elizabeth Maziejka did work on the transcription.
[54]Miller, *The Story of World War II.* 151.

REDEMPTION

[55]"Operation Downfall", *American Experience: Victory in the Pacific.* PBS. www.pbs.org/wgbh/americanexperience/features/general-article/pacific-operation-downfall/
[56] Hillenbrand, Laura. *Unbroken: A World War II Story of Survival, Resilience, and Redemption.* New York: Random House, 2010. 198-199.
[57] This incident is confirmed at "Hanaoka Sendai #7-B", *Center for Research, Allied POWS Under the Japanese.* www.mansell.com/pow_resources/camplists/sendai/sendai_07_hanuoka/hanaoka_7_b.html. Joe Minder's name can also be found on the POW roster there.
[58]Interview with Admiral Stuart S. Murray, U.S. Naval Institute Oral History interview, 1974. "USS Battleship Missouri Memorial", https://ussmissouri.org/learn-the-history/surrender/admiral-murrays-account.

[59] Sides, Hampton. *Ghost Soldiers: The Forgotten Epic Story of World War II's Most Dramatic Mission*. New York: Doubleday, 2001. 329.

RESURRECTION

[60] "World War II-Valor in the Pacific National Monument". National Park Service, U.S. Department of the Interior. http://www.nps.gov/valr/faqs.htm

[61] In late July 2015, as this book went to press, the Defense POW/MIA Accounting Agency began the exhumations of the 388 unidentified victims at the National Memorial Cemetery of the Pacific in Honolulu. Modern forensics should help with the identifying of 80% of the crew.

ADDITIONAL SOURCE NOTES

[62] Interview with Gerald Ross. Interviewed by Matthew Rozell, Hudson Falls High School World War II Living History Project, Veterans' Symposium, May 19, 2001. Also, classroom interview, 1998. Mary Bancroft and Cameron Rigby worked on transcriptions.

[63] Interview with Joseph Fiore. Interviewed by Katelyn Mann, January 13, 2004.

[64] Interview with Dante 'Dan' Orsini. Interviewed by Shea Kolar, Dec. 8, 2005. Also, Mikayla Orsini, Jan. 7, 2012, and classroom interviews.

[65] Source Notes: Minder, Joseph G. World War II Diary of Joseph G. Minder, 1941-1945. Unpublished manuscript. Joe Minder's diary was reformatted in the spring semester of 2015 for use here by my 12th graders as a class project. Alanna Belanger, Sean Daley, Jessica Hogan, Emma Kitchner, Zoe Muller, Brendan Murphy, Ruthie Rainbow, Jack Roche, Nathan Smith, Kylie Tripp, and Alexis Winney all played a role in piecing it together.

[66] Interview with Major Richard M. Gordon-Bataan Death March Survivor. HistoryNet. www.historynet.com/world-war-ii-

interview-with-major-richard-m-gordon-bataan-death-march-survivor.htm. Major Gordon also wrote a well-received memoir titled *Horyo: Memoirs of an American POW*. Saint Paul: Paragon House, 1999.
[67] Burr, Patten. "John Parsons, Local GI, Recounts Jap Tortures", *The Glens Falls Post-Star*, Jan. 30, 1946.
[68] Interview with Dorothy Schechter. Interviewed by Kaitlyn Barbieri and Matthew Rozell, Jan. 5, 2007.
[69] Interview with John Leary. Interviewed by Matthew Rozell, Veterans' Symposium, May 19, 2001.
[70] Interview with Robert Addison, Interviewed by Ayme Baumler, Dec. 6, 2005. Addison commentary also taken from our veteran symposiums, May 19, 2001; May 24, 2002. Sara Prehoda and Jackie Quarters helped with the transcription.
[71] Interview with Gerald West. Interviewed by Laura Heil, Dec. 20, 2005. West commentary also taken from our veteran symposiums, May 19, 2001; May 24, 2002.
[72] Interview with Thomas H. Jones, Interviewed by Phillip Kilmartin, Jan. 16, 2009. Also Ashleigh Fitzgerald, Dec.31, 2009.
[73] Interview with Alvin Peachman, June 16, 2003. Interview by Matthew Rozell. My interview conducted with him at his home occurred 25 years after having had him as my high school history teacher. Shannon Bohan, Naomi Borlang, Kate Mann, and John O'Hara helped with the transcription.
[74] Ralph Leinoff was interviewed on various occasions. He developed close relationships with his student interviewers and his remembrances throughout this book were from interviews with Jillian Casey, Dec. 7, 2010; Matthew Dumas, Jan. 7, 2009; Matthew Rozell, Jan. 14, 2009; and John Trackey, Jan. 2, 2010. In the interview with Jillian Casey, Jillian noted the following: "At the time the bombs were dropped, Mr. Leinoff had four landings in the Pacific and he said he 'wasn't looking to do a fifth one.' He stated that [in 1945] he didn't care what happened to the Japanese. I wasn't expecting what followed: 'Since then, I have questioned—I don't have answers—I have questions about the way it was done, why we had to do it.' "

[75] Interview with Walter Hooke. Interviewed by Anthony Rosa, Jan. 9, 2008.

[76] Interview with Nicholas H. Grinaldo, Interviewed by Michael Aikey, New York State Military Museum, September 26, 2001.

[77] Interview with John A. Sidur. Interviewed by Wayne Clarke, New York State Military Museum, October 1, 2010.

[78] Dan Lawler visited my classroom several times. Lawler's reminisces for this book were also recorded and analyzed by Kristyn Wagner in an interview she did on Dec. 4, 2005, at his home. As a side note, Lawler remembered an incident as they were preparing to land at Peleliu that reminded him of home: "As we left for this island, I boarded a landing ship. There wasn't enough room in the mess hall for all of us, so we ate our meals topside. One afternoon while eating lunch, a friend of mine hollered to me if I was from New York, and I said, 'Yes!' He then asked if I knew where 'Hudson Falls' was. This big machine that we were sitting on was made at the Sandy Hill Iron and Brass Co.; there was a nameplate on the side. It was a big winch. My father helped make this machine! I asked a sailor what it was used for, and he said that after the ship has unloaded, this winch, which was attached to the anchor, would pull the ship off the beach."

[79] John Murray's narrative of his experience on Peleliu has been excerpted from a private letter written to his son in 1995.

[80] James Butterfield and Dan Lawler visited my classroom many times over several years, beginning in May 2000. Their interviews are noted elsewhere in the Notes.

[81] Blakeslee, Robert B. Unpublished interview conducted in 1945.

[82] Interview with Sanford Berkman. Interviewed by Michael Russert and Wayne Clarke for the New York State Military Museum, September 26, 2007. Also, incidental information gleaned from Murphy, Tyler, "WWII Marine commander recalls wounds of Iwo Jima", *The Altamont Enterprise,* July 31, 2013.

[83] Art LaPorte was interviewed on many occasions for this project. Mary Lee Bellosa and Heather Aubrey worked on the Oct. 1998 interview I conducted. He was also interviewed by David

Elliot on Jan. 9, 2004. Childhood memory shared by Katelyn Mann Redus, 2019.

[84] Interview with Herbert Altshuler. Interviewed by Marissa Huntington, Jan. 8, 2012; Mark Ostrander, Fall 2008; Britneigh Sipowitz, Dec. 18, 2010. I also interviewed Herb in 2009.

[85] Source Notes: Doty, Andrew. *Backwards Into Battle: A Tail Gunner's Journey in World War II*. Palo Alto: Tall Tree Press, 1995. Used with author permission.

[86] Interview with Bruce Manell. Interviewed by Kayla Cronin, Dec. 18, 2003.

[87] Interview with Katherine Abbott. Interviewed by Elizabeth Conley, January 11, 2007.

[88] Interview with John Norton. Interviewed by Troy Belden, Jan. 15, 2008. Also, Pekar, Eric. "Granville Then & Now – John Norton, Granville booster." May 26, 2022. NY/VT Media.

[89] Interview with Joseph Marcino. Interviewed by Brooke Goff, Dec. 17, 2004.